BATH ADMINISTER'D

Corporation Affairs
at the 18th-Century Spa

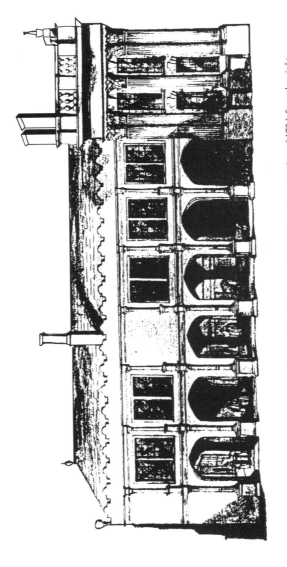

The Stuart Guildhall built over the open Markethouse, with the Georgian extension of 1724-5 on the right. View taken from the west.

BATH ADMINISTER'D

Corporation Affairs
at the 18th-Century Spa

by Trevor Fawcett

RUTON : 2001

*The first thirty pages, said my father, turning over
the leaves - are a little dry...*

*but I doe believe that there is nothing herein
mentioned which may not by chance att one time or
another happen to bee needfull to some person or
another.*

*How these curiosities would be quite forgott, did not
such idle fellowes as I am putt them downe.*

(Sterne, *Tristram Shandy*; Gough, *The History of Myddle*;
Aubrey, *Brief Lives*)

First published in the United Kingdom in 2001 by
RUTON, 25 Northampton Street, Bath, and produced by
R. Milsom & Associates 01454 850033

ISBN 0-9526326-2-4

INTRODUCTION

'The Mayor and Corporation of Bath', the Duchess of Somerset told her son in 1743, 'have published an advertisement in the newspapers, with a reward of twenty pounds [over £1000 today] to whoever will discover some idle people who threw dirt and cabbage stalks at the Duchess of Bedford as she was crossing the Abbey Green there.' The authorities could hardly ignore such an affront to the dignity of a valued client and to the city's own reputation for law and order. Sound local government mattered in any eighteenth-century town, but at a fashionable health resort the stakes were raised by the presence and favour of rank and riches. And if a well-regulated environment was seen as a priority, the role of the Corporation became paramount. True, it was private enterprise that furnished many of the amenities the spa trade needed - transportation, inns and lodgings, an endless supply of goods and services, medical expertise, and a constant round of amusements. These were certainly prerequisites if Bath was to stay ahead of its competitors, but underlying them all lay a framework of

governance that ultimately centred on the ancient office of Mayor and derived from Bath's legal status as a corporate borough with freedoms dating back centuries.

This book examines Georgian Bath through a rather unfamiliar lens then, the view from the Guildhall. It shows how the Elizabethan Charter and subsequent Acts of Parliament invested the Corporation with considerable powers while restricting those powers to the narrow limits of the Bath Liberties. It explains too how authority was shared at times with other institutions such as the Somerset magistrates, the parish Vestries, the various bodies of Commissioners, and, up to a point, the city freemen and the trade companies. Altogether over a hundred topics are covered, including every Corporation office and all areas of municipal responsibility - from managing the water supply, street lighting and rubbish removal to collecting rents and rates, licensing pubs, and inspecting weights and measures. The Council ran the historic hot baths, supervised the provisions market, administered a large portfolio of properties, and coped with an increasingly complex financial operation that required high levels of borrowing. It often found itself involved in negotiations with large landowners, in petitions to Parliament, and in expensive litigation. An oligarchic, self-perpetuating body of ten Aldermen, twenty Councilmen and one Recorder, the Corporation alone elected the city M.P.s, decided which of its number should hold which office, and appointed the Town Clerk, the Rector of Bath, the Master of the Grammar School, and many lesser officers - from the Sergeants-at-Arms and the Pumper (important characters nonetheless) down to the humble custodian of the town's weighing machine. Equally important, the Bath authorities supplied the magistrates' bench, presided over several courts of justice, and administered the city gaol. On their highest dignity they consorted with royalty itself. Yet while there was ample scope for political opportunism, the city fathers acquitted themselves none too badly by the standards of the time.

Nepotism and lack of accountability were perhaps their worst sins.

The Corporation and its members were associated or entangled in various ways with other significant organisations and interests within contemporary Bath society. A number of these links have seemed worth recognising by specific entries in this book. Notable among them are the sections on Master Tradesmen, Journeymen, and Apprentices, and their related institutions - the Trade Companies, the Freemen, the Freemasons, and the Friendly Societies. Other entries focus on the more independent organisations - Canal Companies, Infirmaries, Militias and Volunteers, and Turnpike Trusts - and special attention is paid to those flamboyant despots of the spa scene, the Masters of Ceremonies.

Altogether this is a story rich in detail. It tells of tithingmen and Sunday schools, of elections and processioning, of fire engines and gilded maces, of weighing loaves of bread and the misappropriation of land. It lists the succession of M.P.s, of Town Criers, of Rectors of Walcot. It recounts how one Guildhall decayed and another rose in its place. It features the Abbey organist (and his organ blower) as well as Jane Austen's aunt, and at one moment the ornamental town swans sail into view. Should you be curious to learn what Sir Thomas White's money was used for? why Ralph Allen raised a troop of uniformed guardsmen? who died on a Bath gallows in 1780? or how many residents paid duty on hair powder in 1795? - you need only enquire within.

This book in sum offers a mass of fresh, reliable information in an accessible format. It can be read straight through for its own intrinsic interest, casually dipped into, or used for quick reference and as a springboard for further inquiry. For ease of consultation a dictionary style of presentation has been adopted, i.e. an alphabetical sequence of entries with appropriate cross-references to help place the topic in a wider context.

N.B. Pre-1752 dates are always given in 'new style', i.e. 28 Jan 1726/7 is regarded as occurring in 1727. Certain entries quote sums of money. To obtain very approximate modern equivalents multiply by around sixty - though because relative values have changed this will sometimes understate, sometimes overstate, the true comparison.

Abbey Church (St Peter and Paul's)

The main focus of Corporate worship since the late 16th century, the Abbey was where civic and sacred came together, where the city fathers knelt to the established church. Its Gothic dignity always impressed newcomers even if they did sometimes blink at finding rows of shops nestled against the buttresses and the nave being used as a general meeting place. Hidden behind a bulky central screen and organ gallery, the chancel was fitted up with pews and benches for services. Under the great east window stood Wade's marble altarpiece (donated by Bath's popular M.P. in 1726) and on the south side, facing the pulpit, the Corporation's cushioned pew with another for aldermen's wives. A Mayor's pew was ordered for newly enlarged St James's church in 1718, but the Abbey was far more convenient, an easy step from the Guildhall for the robed Corporation to walk to service. The Aldermen may have worshipped there most Sundays, with a fuller civic turnout on red-letter days like the induction of the Mayor (October) and anniversary of the Restoration (29 May), and on special patriotic occasions - coronations, victory thanksgivings, and solemn fasts and humiliations. When John Penrose, a visiting parson, preached in the Abbey at Whitsuntide 1766, he noted approvingly that the Aldermen (a 'pompous' sight in their scarlet gowns) made a point of taking the sacrament, so professing publicly their Anglican allegiance. From time to time the Rector of Bath would deliver one of the 'gift' sermons the Corporation paid him extra for. In fact, holding the advowson, they appointed the Rector to his living in the first place, just as they chose the organist, administered the charitable 'Lent bread' bequest (and a similar fund for church repairs), stored fire appliances in the north transept, flew the flag from the tower, gave the sexton his Christmas box, and generally treated the Abbey as their own. Cooperation between Guildhall and Vestry would have been vital over many matters, including the building's use for charity concerts or the massive Sunday School services in the 1780s, and similarly over the establishment in 1798 of a better choir than the Bluecoats children had hitherto provided, and to which the Corporation contributed. In a further gesture, the city sometimes paid towards the cost of beating (i.e. perambulating) the Abbey parish bounds.

••• See also **Organist of the Abbey Church; Parish Administration; Rector of Bath.**

Acts of Parliament

The Elizabethan Charter guaranteed the Corporation's essential rights, but a series of special Bath Acts conferred important additional powers. These local Acts were typically initiated by the Corporation, lobbied for as necessary in London, and submitted to Parliament by the city's M.P.s. The ten 'Bath' Bills enacted between 1707 and 1801 are identified below by the monarch's 'regnal year' (e.g. 6 Geo III = 6th year of George III's reign) followed by the chapter and date of the Act.

> *6 Anne c.42 (1707/08)* was a hybrid Act that set up a new institution, the Bath Turnpike Trust, and also initiated a sequence of legislation to 'improve' Bath by giving the Corporation certain legal rights over public space. On the one hand it established an independent 'Justice Trust' with the right to farm traffic tolls to pay for the repair and upkeep of the highways leading in and out of Bath. On the other it granted the Corporation control of the city streets as regards pitching and paving, street cleaning and rubbish removal, illumination (at this date by candle lanterns and oil lamps), and the licensing of up to sixty sedan or bath chairs.
>
> *7 Geo I c.19 (1720/21)* extended these provisions for a further 21 years, slightly amended the Turnpike Trust, and required the sedan chairmen to wait for customers at agreed chair stands.
>
> *12 Geo II c.20 (1739)* enlarged the previous two Acts, permitted the Turnpike Trust to borrow up to £3000 on the tolls, charged the cost of various services (surveyors, scavengers, watchmen and beadles) to a local rate of up to 8d in the pound, and laid down a tariff for hiring chairs. It introduced a new element of policing by giving watchmen and beadles the duty of arresting vagabonds, malefactors and disorderly persons.
>
> *30 Geo II c.65 (1757)* no longer spoke of turnpiking which was covered instead by 30 Geo II c.67 (1757) and a series of subsequent Turnpike

Acts. It did, however, update the street legislation and placed the onus on parish Vestries to appoint surveyors to collect the rates and employ street-cleaners and lamplighters, even though the city magistrates still determined where lamps should be fixed and what hours they should be lit. The Act further stipulated that buildings should be fitted with drainpipes, banned noisy coal carts from the town centre at night, and tried to stop the poor from scavenging at rubbish dumps.

6 Geo III c.16 (1766) established a Court of Requests 'for the more easy and speedy Recovery of small Debts within the City of Bath' and named the initial bench of fifty Commissioners who were eligible to sit with members of the Corporation to adjudicate cases.

6 Geo III c.70 (1766) was a major Act with a triple thrust. First, it sought to alleviate congestion and improve air circulation in the old city centre by widening certain streets, doing away with the numerous hanging shop signs (flat signboards being allowed instead), and relocating the provisions market away from its traditional obstructive site in the High Street. Second, it settled a controversial issue: how much of the municipal water supply was due to the private Kingston Estate. Third, and most important of all, it removed the duties of street cleaning, lighting and policing from individual parishes and vested them in a new body of twenty Commissioners appointed jointly by the Corporation and the four parishes. Paralleling similar developments in other English towns, this marked a key stage in the evolution of local government since it introduced a fresh tier of administration and consolidated the former parish street rates into a single fund.

9 Geo III c.95 (1769) allowed the trustees of the Pulteney Estate to acquire land for the approaches to the intended Pulteney Bridge, granted certain

Bathwick springs to Bath, and extended the city's jurisdiction over a small strip of Bathwick near the river.

29 Geo III c.73 (1789) encountered more local opposition than any previous legislation, mainly because it raised turnpike tolls by some 50% in order to finance large-scale city improvements. The Turnpike Trustees voiced their protest, as did coal suppliers, farmers, and many householders, but despite much petitioning against the Bill it passed in June 1789 and ushered in a six-year phase of inner city renewal which included building the Private Baths and the new Pump Room, creating five new streets, and widening others. The Act scheduled properties that were to be pulled down or altered (at a cost of at least £83,000 in compensation), and it named the special body of Improvement Commissioners to oversee the whole operation.

33 Geo III c.89 (1793) was strictly speaking not a city Act, since its sponsors were prominent residents of outer Walcot, i.e. the considerable part of the parish outside Bath proper which came under the formal jurisdiction of Bathforum and thus far lacked any statutory street controls and policing powers. Though late in coming, this Act was more specific on many points than any of its predecessors and offered a useful model for the subsequent Acts for Bathwick (1801) and Bath itself (1814). As with the Act of 1766, the legislation for outer Walcot set up a supervisory body of Commissioners - solid men of financial substance who were empowered to act as magistrates. As usual its provisions covered street paving and cleansing, refuse removal, lighting, policing, and the regulation of porters, sedan chairs, and (in case they were needed) hackney cabs, but other clauses touched on matters often left formerly to bylaws. For instance the Act included sections that banned letting off fireworks or playing football in the streets, or trundling wheelbarrows along pavements. It required houses to be numbered, and bulldogs and mastiffs to be muzzled out of doors, and it prescribed on many other details.

41 Geo III c.126 (1801) gave statutory powers to all Bathwick outside the Bath Liberties. Minor changes apart, it followed the Walcot Act closely and provided Bathwick with its own Commissioners from this date.

Besides these ten Improvement Acts, Parliament from time to time passed other local legislation affecting Bath. These further Acts were to do with the Avon Navigation (1712), the General Hospital (1738, 1779), the Theatre (1768), Pulteney Bridge (1772, 1799), the Kennet & Avon Canal (1794, 1796, 1798, 1801), and the Turnpikes (seven specific local Acts between 1757 and 1801).

••• See also **Bathwick**; **Canal Companies**; **Infirmaries**; **Parliament**; **Turnpike Trusts**.

Aldermen

The Corporation's senior echelon - and the fact that around 1760 the combined ages of the nine Aldermen then serving exceeded 700 years indicates just how senior. Aldermen did sometimes resign, but most died in office. All had risen through the ranks of Councilman, Constable and Bailiff before being considered for elevation to this higher plane. The Chamberlain commonly, and the Mayor virtually always, was an Alderman, and Aldermen alone supplied the magistrates' bench until the new Charter of 1794 at last allowed Councilmen to serve as well. What distinguished them on civic occasions was their scarlet robes - self-provided, it seems. The elder Pitt, one of the city M.P.s, once imagined himself as such a dignatory enthroned - feeling, he remarked, 'like an alderman of Bath' as he sat in his great chair. Most likely it was his old political ally Ralph Allen or his current aldermanic friend E.B.Collibee that he had in mind.

Ale Tasters see Supervisors

Almshouses

Bath possessed two mediaeval foundations for the old and infirm, St John's and St Catherine's, plus the ancient leper house of St Mary Magdalen in Holloway, which in the 18th century housed a very few 'idiot' paupers and each year received £1.8s. (Queen Elizabeth's charity) from the city. Earlier, St John's Hospital and the Magdalen, both Priory possessions, had survived the Dissolution of 1539. In 1572 the patronage of St John's passed from the Crown to Bath Corporation, who henceforth appointed the Master in charge, and for a time (1617-62) even entrusted the post to various mayors or aldermen in order to retain a tight grip on the valuable St John's estate in Bath and beyond. A persistent claim that the Corporation had in fact usurped this estate was finally settled by recourse to the law in 1713, when the charity arrangements were systematised and the estate tenancies re-let. In future the Master, always a clergyman, was to manage the establishment himself and decide which of the poor elderly citizens (six women, six men) who applied for a room were most worthy. Instead of it being the City Chamberlain's job, it was now up to him to handle Hospital income and dole out specified weekly allowances to the almsfolk, supply their blue gowns (worn at twice-daily chapel services), and cover the costs of laundry, nursing, and general maintenance. With overall supervision for St John's now vested in the Lord Chancellor and others, the Corporation found itself reduced merely to choosing at rare intervals a new Master (usually from the Chapman family) and to financing the rebuild of the dilapidated chapel in 1717. Hence John Wood's remodelling of the site for the Duke of Chandos in 1727-30 was not their concern.

They also lost their say over the other almshouse, St Catherine's. Sometimes called the Black Alms (from the colour of the residents' gowns), this 15th-century hospice in Bimbury Lane was the very earliest municipal charity, once associated with the guild chantry of St Catherine in Stalls Church. It had escaped confiscation under the 1547 Chantries Act, and in 1552, along with the Grammar School, had been endowed with a more than adequate income from city properties to support ten poor citizens. But over the next two centuries the city fathers so muddled the accounts and so obscured which properties were to support the endowment that the Charity Commisssioners' inquiry of 1734-5 could identify only five of them. It therefore indicted the Corporation for maladministration, denied them future management of St Catherine's, and set up a board of trustees, among them the Bishop of Bath and Wells and the Rector of Bath. The change did not affect the ten beneficiaries of the charity. Like their counterparts in St John's, each resident (all men at this period) had his own room, a living allowance of sixpence a day and a new black gown every two years, both paid for by the Corporation from charitable bequests. Since Stalls Church had long since gone, they attended worship at the Abbey Church and so were probably more noticeable about town than the blue-gowners of St John's.

••• See also **Infirmaries**; **Private Estates**.

••• **List of Masters of St John's Hospital 1700-1800**: *William Clement 1683-1711; John Chapman 1711-37; Walter Chapman 1737-91; John Chapman 1791-1816.*

Apprentices

To qualify as a city freeman usually meant serving a full local apprenticeship in which boys were 'bound', by contract, to a qualified working freeman for seven years starting around the age of fourteen. The term laid down for the few enrolled girls tended to be shorter - three to five years - typically served in some occupation to do with fashion. In the 71-year period 1706-76, over 1500 boys and 23 girls were recorded as 'indentured' in this way, though the official list is probably incomplete. Furthermore many other adolescents must have been bound by private verbal agreement. These apprentices too boarded with their employer to learn a trade (especially domestic service) but never became enrolled freemen. The Corporation's register of apprentices, for long a vital proof of the future right to trade in the city, reveals marked fluctuations in new entrants - averaging well over 30 a year in 1707-09, 1734-37, and the peak decade of 1751-60, but less that half that in the 1720s, 1740s, or after 1763 when apprenticeships steadily tailed off once the freemen lost their trading monopoly.

Indentures were a statutory safeguard binding on both parties. The master, standing *in loco parentis*, promised that his apprentice would be properly accommodated, fed, clothed, and freely instructed in the business concerned. The apprentice undertook in return to serve his master loyally, 'keep his secrets', and neither marry, nor gamble, nor frequent public houses during his specified term. The printed contract had to be registered and sealed at the Guildhall and government duty paid on the premium, i.e. the fee required by the master from parent or guardian (or Charity School trustees) before an apprenticeship began. These fees varied enormously according to the reputation of the master and the status of his occupation. Around 1770 one Bath gardener charged a mere guinea, a barber-and-wigmaker 10 guineas, cabinet makers from 14 guineas to £40, haberdashers, mercers and drapers £50-£100, apothecaries around 100 guineas, and a leading Hospital surgeon (Henry Wright) a stupendous 250 guineas. Not every apprenticeship ran its course however. Masters sometimes fell ill, died, or failed in their duty of care and instruction. Apprentices sometimes misbehaved, found they disliked the trade, proved unreliable, or even absconded. As they approached manhood, a few found the constraints intolerable. Such cases came before the Bath magistrates and were then adjudicated at Quarter Sessions, often resulting in an apprentice's transfer to another master to serve out his time. But household and employment arrangements generally worked well enough. In some cases affectionate family-like bonds developed, and of course some apprentices were contracted to their own fathers and other relatives. The more useful an apprentice's contribution to the workplace became, the greater the inducement to reward him with a regular wage. A master might accept a string of pupil employees over the years - the shoemaker Philip Palmer, for example, had around 15 apprentices at different times and the keeper of the *Bear* inn, Joseph Phillott, 16 or more. For certain trades it is possible to trace lineages, as former apprentices became partners and masters and in due course took on apprentices of their own. These links, plus the fact that some 95% of those indentured were recruited from Bath itself, lent cohesion to the body of Bath freemen that many of them duly became. In the 1790s apprentices joined the freemen in their symbolic perambulations of Bath Common and shared in the cakes, if not the ale, at the end of the ceremony.

••• See also **Journeymen**; **Freemen**; **Master Tradesmen**.

Archdeacon of Bath see Diocese of Bath and Wells; Rector of Bath

Archives

Corporation papers and documents were housed in the Guildhall, mostly in the care of the Town Clerk. They included the precious collection of charters and grants (the basic proofs of Bath's corporate identity), former administrative records, documentation of current Corporation business, and large numbers of property deeds. Crucial items like money bonds had to be kept specially secure - in a chest under four keys according to one early bylaw. The older material was of more than historic interest and had to be referred to not infrequently in cases of dispute. Council books and even the Elizabethan Charter (insured for £100) were taken up to London, carefully packed in wool, in 1704 for use in legal evidence, and the Charter again in 1785. A Council minute of 1734 asked for all the ancient charters and grants to be sent to London for translation into English, and in 1751 it was agreed that three Council members should assist in 'methodizing all papers and writing belonging to this Corporation'. Little came of that until 1775-7 when first John Furman and then John Pacey were employed to abstract and index the English and Latin property deeds and other items, some of the documents being sent to London in a painted box. It was embarrassing when records were found to be deficient. Council books went missing in 1704. The House of Lords' solicitor withheld deeds belonging to St John's Hospital in 1712. Other deeds had strayed by 1779-81, and the disgraced former Deputy Chamberlain, Thomas Baldwin, had to be sued in 1792 for the return of ratebooks and other papers. Besides documents in manuscript the archive contained printed works on law and administration, including statutes in force, mostly shelved in the Town Clerk's office. There were also local maps and perhaps copies of the *London Gazette* which the Guildhall subscribed to. In the old building the charters and the city seal were kept in a special cupboard drawer, and bundles of paid bills in the municipal chest, but the new Guildhall of 1777 contained a properly fireproof Record Room with lettered and numbered drawers for documents. In addition the Mayor kept a set of reference works in his room for use by the magistrates.

••• See also **Regalia and Symbols**.

Assize Courts see Somerset Assizes and Sessions

Assize of Bread

The Mayor's right to hold an Assize of Bread (i.e. to decide the price or weight of baked loaves, the staple of diet) was enshrined in the Charter. Some towns sold standard sizes of loaf whose selling price fluctuated according to the cost of grain and flour. Bath preferred the alternative of standardising *prices* - from the penny loaf up to monsters costing 18d - but varying the *weight*, a method which allowed finer tuning to prevailing wheat prices but also demanded a closer watch on bakers to prevent customers receiving short measure. Bread Assizes could be held as often as required, weekly, monthly or at much longer intervals, and bakers simply had to adjust to the changes announced by the Mayor or Deputy Clerk of the Market and based on the bushel price at Bristol and (from 1768 or earlier) at Devizes averaged with Warminster. At times this involved dispatching a Beadle specially to Bristol or Devizes, but eventually the Devizes Town Crier was paid a fee to keep the Corporation informed. Further complications arose from the local preference for the 9-gallon corn bushel, the leeway permitted by the 'baking allowance', and the making of bread in three different qualities - so that, for example, the Assize of 27 May 1767 specified that *penny* loaves stamped W (white), WH (wheaten) or H (household, i.e. wholemeal) should weigh respectively 6oz 2dr, 8oz 3dr, and 10oz 11dr, with dearer loaves in proportion. When grain harvests were poor, the size of loaves at Bath would shrink noticeably. The authorities then checked bakers with extra vigilance and imposed deterrent fines for selling under weight. During serious scarcities (e.g. 1795-6 and 1799-1801) they banned the baking of the more luxurious white bread altogether, and in August 1800 experimented with standardising the weight of loaves rather than the price, at least for quartern sizes. The bakers were now complaining bitterly about the Assize and wanted it fixed partly by the new toll-free Saturday corn market at Bath (from February 1800). The Corporation deemed this to be too much under the bakers' influence and, finding that setting no Assize at all only drove up bread prices, turned again to Bristol whose flour prices were held down by American imports. In 1801 the bakers, still aggrieved, refused to cooperate with the Cooperation and took their case to law.

Avon Navigation see Canal Companies

Bailiffs

Somerset resembled other shire counties in having an office of High Sheriff answerable directly to the Crown, with a Bailiff acting under him, but the incorporated borough of Bath had long since freed itself from the High Sheriff's interference and adopted the titles Sheriff and Bailiff for its own purposes. At Bath, unusually, the two offices were combined and the titles used almost interchangeably, except that 'Sheriff' retained its more authoritative, county flavour and was preferred when the judicial nature of the office needed emphasis, while 'Bailiff' related directly to their bailiwick, i.e. the Liberties of Bath from which the county High Sheriff was excluded. Each year two Bailiffs were elected out of the body of Councilmen, normally the same pair who had acted as Constables the previous year but one. Election was indeed partly a reward for having so acted, for whereas Constables went unpaid the Bailiffs could profit handsomely from office - unlike a London Sheriff, say, whose expenses might be severe. By tradition the Bailiffs held the lease of the provisions market and the biannual Bath fairs, and they paid an annual rent to the city for this lucrative right to hire out stalls and standings. Between 1700 and 1736 the rent more than doubled from £30 to £80, but the way in which it leapt to £360 in 1776 once the market had been improved and enlarged, and then to £420 by 1787, demonstrates just how valuable the privilege could be, even after payment of overheads for rates, repairs, cleaning and supervision. (In 1761 and 1775 their rent rose to £120 and then to £160 for a different reason, namely the reduction and then the ending of the Bailiffs' obligation to provide Corporation feasts.) In addition to hiring out stalls and charging tolls on basket retailers, the Bailiffs' supervisory role entailed checking for illegal trading, controlling porters and basketwomen, dealing with complaints, and sometimes temporarily banning produce from sale - as in autumn 1792 when 'old salmon' was prohibited for several weeks. The Supervisors of Flesh and Fish had a role here too, but the Bailiffs' chief auxiliary from 1767 was a Deputy Clerk and Constable of the Market.

In their other principal sphere of activity - court proceedings and custody of prisoners - the Bailiffs again made use of deputies, though they attended court in person. For the execution of writs and other legal processes they relied on the Town Clerk and probably allowed him their fees in return. They presumably turned to parish constables for the summoning of juries, another of their duties. They could charge debtors set sums on their arrest and imprisonment, and they farmed out the city Prison to a Gaoler of their own choosing, taking care to safeguard themselves from personal financial liability by first obtaining a money bond from the Gaoler's guarantors. Ultimately they were responsible to the Corporation for all custodial matters, including the safe transport of prisoners between Bath and the county gaols for which they sometimes paid the cost of armed escorts. Bailiffs were seldom aldermen, yet their roles gave them an authority that fitted them when required to represent the Corporation and borough in place of the Mayor. It was the Bailiffs, for instance, who waited on the royal princes in 1738, 1761 and 1765 to offer them the freedom of the city, who presented William Pitt with his freedom in 1757, who formally thanked Ralph Allen for his services in 1763, and who accompanied the Mayor, Chamberlain and Town Clerk to Cheltenham in 1788 in order to invite George III to visit Bath.

••• See also **Court of Piedpoudre**; **Court of Record**; **Fairs**; **Gaoler**; **Market**.

Banks

The Corporation transacted much of its business in cash. Before the 1770s, whenever it did require bill-broking services, it probably turned to established London houses rather than risk the early small-scale operators at Bath. In 1768, however, the Bath Bank opened, followed by the Bath & Somersetshire Bank (1775) and the Bath City Bank (1776), each formed by a consortium of substantial local businessmen with connections throughout the region. The Corporation would still have been wary - and with good reason. Regulation of country banks was minimal. Provided they had the capital and collateral, any partnership could form a bank and issue paper currency without hindrance, scrutiny or official declaration of reserves. By reinvesting their clients' deposits they might turn a good profit, but they stood totally liable if public confidence in the bank or the system wavered. Increasingly, though, the Chamberlain's office must have been handling drafts and bills of exchange. Some of its lenders were drawing on local banks. So the city was pulled in. By 1780 the accounts reveal payments to the clerks of both the Bath Bank and the Bath & Somersetshire, and ten years later the Bath Bank was handling the accounts of the municipally run New Private Baths. When the crash came in 1793, the Bath Bank held firm, but two others went to the wall owing the Corporation money - the Bath City Bank just 15 guineas, the Bath & Somersetshire a more serious £508 (of which £152 was recovered in a dividend pay-off c.1799). The crisis of 1793-4 brought down many other enterprises at Bath and speculative building programmes - essentially sustained by loans and credit - came almost to a halt. More robustly financed, the Corporation's own public works went on to completion.

Bathforum see County Administration

Baths and Pump Rooms

The Corporation were merely custodians of the hot springs, since these belonged in a larger sense to the whole nation. At the same time it was obvious - and had been since the 16th century - that access to the spa for the vast majority must be rationed. The well-to-do could be welcomed with open arms for they brought custom and paid handsomely for their keep and treatment. The rest were received on sufferance, and then only if sponsored, licensed and approved. Most of the Corporation's attention inevitably focused on the first sort.

Gilmore's Bath map of 1694 illustrates the five open-air baths - the joint King's and Queen's baths near the town centre, and the Cross, Hot and Lepers' baths served by separate springs in a group further west. At this date facilities for water drinking, an increasingly modish therapy, were primitive enough, and the royal visits of 1702-3 further exposed their limitations. In 1705-6 therefore the Corporation, rather boldly, replaced old buildings just north of the King's Bath with an elegant, large-windowed Pump Room perfect for polite morning socialising (to a backdrop of music playing 8-10 a.m.) and fitted up for drinking in style. Expensive it might have been, but it gave the spa an edge on rivals and helped extend the visiting season well into autumn. By the 1720s the Pump Room already seemed too small. A 'vast crowd' thronged it in September 1723 and a decade later John Wood estimated it could hold barely a third of the smart company it was

meant for. Though his own plan for a second storey was rejected, the addition of a musicians' gallery in 1734 created some extra room, and together with new pumps installed at the Hot Bath in 1743 and in the Cross Bath gallery five years later, this tided the Corporation over until 1751 when a costly extra bay was added on the west side. The expense of compensation, demolition, and building of this extension exceeded many times the Pumper's rental and shows how much the Pump Room was then valued.

Improvements of the baths themselves came more slowly. The gentry long favoured the relatively private Cross Bath, which had the coolest waters and a gallery from which musicians (the City Waits?) at times serenaded the bathers. But apart from stabilising the carved stone centrepiece in the 1740s and renewing the drinking pump, the Corporation undertook no major works there until Baldwin's and Palmer's massive reorganisations of 1783-4 and 1797-8 in which the Cross Bath was freed from encumbering houses and became an eyecatching terminal to new Bath Street. The more humdrum Hot Bath had lost its south gallery in 1732 and was modified in 1742 when the General Hospital gained use of it for two hours each morning.

Eventually in 1775-8 the younger John Wood rebuilt the whole structure, and the Corporation appointed not the Sergeants-at-Arms but one of their own number, the surgeon John Symons, to manage the now upgraded establishment - an arrangement that lasted until 1787 when the existing staff were dismissed and a Council committee took control. Meanwhile the King's and Queen's baths had undergone various piecemeal changes and repairs, including improvement of the entrance slips and dry pumping areas on the advice of joint committees of the Council and resident Bath physicians. Much greater upheaval was caused by the great reconstruction and enlargement of the Pump Room in 1790-5, first under Baldwin and then Palmer on behalf of the Improvement Commissioners - a massive, if ultimately questionable, gesture of confidence in the continued magnetic pull of the waters and the profits they would generate. An important by-product of the scheme was the New Private Baths building in Stall Street. Opened in 1792 under the supervision of one of the Sergeants-at-Arms, this municipal venture might be regarded as the city's second challenge to the privately run Abbey (Kingston) Baths, the first having been the rebuilt Hot Bath in 1778. The Council mostly left the private sector to run the various cold baths, e.g. the long-established Greenway establishment in Widcombe. In 1779 it did agree to install a cold reservoir at the Hot Bath, but that was to temper the water there. Tepid water also supplied the horse bath in Stall Street (c.1793), since it used the waste from the King's Bath.

Bringing in a general tariff of fees was a fairly late innovation. Formerly a voluntary system of clients' tips or 'acknowledgements' had prevailed for paying the staffs of the various city baths and pumps. The Corporation appointed a Pumper to manage the drinking pumps and pump rooms, and two Sergeants to supervise the public baths. Far from being paid, Pumpers were charged a hefty rent for their profitable position. The Sergeants were salaried only from 1783 when their financial losses had become evident following the revival of the Hot Bath. Other employees were also rewarded by gratuities - drinking pump assistants, clothwomen, and the numerous bath guides who accompanied patients into the baths and who (for a fee) worked the wet and dry pumps. In 1719 as many as 11 male and 16 female guides were employed at the four main baths - 'clownish fellowes & ugly old Witches' in one unflattering portrait some years later. It was stipulated in 1737 that guides should wear distinguishing tasselled caps besides the regulation bathing dress of linen drawers and waistcoat for men and a 'decent shift' for women (which bathers themselves could hire or buy). Patients spent about twenty minutes in the water on average but the guides were in and out all day and, according to one observer, looked 'sodden and parboil'd' - yet most kept the job for many years (one female guide for almost fifty years). From time to time the Council took a fresh look at the baths. In 1752-3 for example, having extended the Pump Room, they built dry pumping rooms at the King's Bath, refurbished it, laid ten tons of sea pebbles, reintroduced coal fires, and very briefly experimented with separate bathing times for men and women by alternating King's and Queen's with Cross and Hot baths. It was just at this moment that the city fathers were alarmed to be informed by Charles Lucas, a visiting apothecary who had analysed the mineral waters, that they contained no sulphur, hitherto proclaimed a vital ingredient. This unwelcome finding was soon neutralised, however, by a reinterpretation of the term 'sulphureous', and in the end there was little loss of public confidence in the waters' miraculous virtues and their suitability for a long list of ailments (running to six pages in one Bath guidebook). By 1784 treatments at the King's Bath included vapour baths and electric shock therapy, though none of these special procedures came cheaply. Even general bathing (including costume and towel) cost 1s.6d. a time on top of dues to the guide (1s.), clothwoman (3d.) and Sergeant (3d.).

••• See also **Pumper**; **Sergeants-at-Arms**.

Bathwick

According to a visitor of 1743, Bathwick was still a place of market gardens and pleasure plots, a favourite resort of Bathonians who crossed to it by ferry or came the longer way via Bath Bridge. The village itself comprised little more than a small church, a cluster of houses, a watermill and, close by, the new attraction of Spring Gardens. Appearances deceived however. In 1727, having unexpectedly acquired the 600-acre manor of Bathwick, William Pulteney had begun consolidating leaseholds to prepare for wholesale development at some future date. Forty years later the work was three-quarters done, and the estate's chief trustee, William Johnstone Pulteney, opened negotiations with the Corporation about building a second Bath bridge, the key to exploiting the whole area. In 1769, by

Act of Parliament, he conceded them limited jurisdiction over parts of Bathwick (perhaps seldom exercised) as well as valuable rights to water sources, and in exchange for help over an access route to the bridge on the city side (the future Bridge Street) provided a plot on his own side for the new Prison. This was mutually beneficial, but the Corporation could not accept without protest Pulteney's revised design for a bridge lined with shops, and resisted still more his intention to create a turnpike road between Bathford and Bathwick. Had this been built, it would clearly have creamed traffic off the London Road and, in time, affected city plans to finance improvement works through increased road tolls. Pulteney Bridge, vastly expensive, opened in 1774, but the grand suburb envisaged for Bathwick went unrealised for nearly fifteen years. When the project did get under way, the long-protracted French wars ensured that only a fraction of the scheme was ever implemented. Enough, however, was built and populated by 1801 to require a special Police Act for Bathwick, similar to Walcot's and with the usual provision of Commissioners to oversee its general administration.

••• See also **Liberties of Bath**; **Prisons (City)**; **Private Estates**; **Processioning**.

••• **List of Lords of Bathwick Manor**: *William Cappel, 3rd Earl of Essex 1710?-27; William Pulteney (1st Earl of Bath from 1742) 1727-64; General Harry Pulteney 1764-7; Frances Johnstone Pulteney 1767-82; Henrietta Laura Pulteney (Baroness Bath from 1792, Countess of Bath from 1803) 1782-1808.*

Beadles

The word 'beadle' equally applied to a parish constable, or to wardens and messengers of various kinds (e.g. at the General Hospital), but is here used for a Mayor's officer with policing and court responsibilities. At Bath the position seems originally to have been combined with that of 'Hayward' or supervisor of the Town Common, and subsequently with the job of Town Crier. By 1737, though, there was business enough to occupy two Beadles full-time, from 1764 three, and then from 1782 four - by which time one of the Beadles, John Mackenzie, acted also as a Sergeant-at-Arms. Presumably by intent one Beadle then came from each parish. They were paid a weekly salary which rose from about 6s. in 1737 to 9s. in 1765, 15s. in

1792, and a guinea in 1801, well above rates of inflation and often supplemented by tips. As official servants of His Worshipful the Mayor, they were issued every year with livery coats and laced hats. One or more Beadles would normally be on duty at the Guildhall to deal with visitors and safeguard the Council offices - especially on licensing and rent days. They had a distinct role in conveying prisoners between the Guildhall and city gaol or from Bath to the Shepton Mallet Bridewell and other places. Other out-of-town expeditions might take them to the county assizes, or to Bristol and Devizes to check current corn prices. In 1754 they could be found keeping the boisterous sedan chairmen in order at evening assemblies, and for such additional duties they might be paid extra. Two Beadles were rewarded with five guineas each for their vigilant efforts during the Gordon Riots of 1780, and one of them received a special payment for helping to seize illegal EO gaming tables. Whipping vagrants and criminals also came within their scope, a punishment sometimes administered on top of a cart the better to gratify onlookers. More mundanely Beadles rounded up street beggars, served judicial writs, guarded the courtroom, occasionally inspected shop weights and measures, and generally did the magistrates' bidding.

Bellmen

Up to c.1720 the Chamberlain's accounts occasionally mention providing new coats for the two bellmen. One of these officials (employed by the Bailiffs?) probably rang the trading hours in the market until the Town Crier assumed this function. The other was a night watchman appointed to patrol the streets, call or ring the hours, and alert the town if a fire broke out. This post disappeared with the organisation of a more elaborate parish watch from 1738.

Bellott's Hospital see Infirmaries

Bellringers

The teams of ringers at the Abbey, St James's and - from 1759 - St Michael's created a merry enough din whenever important, tip-dispensing visitors arrived in town, but they also had more official duties in summoning the faithful to worship and pealing messages of civic joy across the rooftops. Every year the very loyal bells rang out to celebrate those key dates of the Protestant monarchy, 5 November and 29 May, and to salute the anniversary of the Coronation and up to half-a-dozen royal birthdays. Whenever royal visitors came to Bath the jubilant clamour increased markedly, as it did too in wartime at news of allied victories and eventual declarations of peace. For all these commissioned peals the Corporation typically paid the sets of ringers fifteen shillings a time, but never salaried them as it did the Waits.

Benefit Societies see Friendly Societies

Bishop see Diocese of Bath and Wells

Bluecoats School see Schools

Bridewell

The Bath Bridewell, sometimes called a 'house of correction', was less a gaol than a workhouse - though one that had barred windows. Hence it came under the J.P.s rather than the Bailiffs. It had been built 1632-35 by converting a barn and stable (near the site of the later Bluecoats School) specifically 'for the settling of poore people on worke' and saving on parish relief. Let to a succession of tenants, it may seldom have served its forced labour purpose since productivity in bridewells was notoriously low, work intermittent, and the whole set-up barely economic. Bridewell keepers can have made little profit out of the paupers, sturdy beggars and vagabonds committed there. In 1733 the Corporation thought of building a new bridewell on Town Acre, but in the end left the problem of the local work-shy and indigent for the parishes to deal with, while trying to remove obvious vagrants in other ways. Any later reference to 'Bridewell' in Bath records usually refers to the county institution at Shepton Mallet.

••• See also **Poorhouses; Prisons (County); Social Problems**.

Bylaws

Charters and statutes provided the framework of administration, whereas bylaws added the fine detail and in some important areas (e.g. policing, rateable services, traffic control) eventually became incorporated in local Acts of Parliament which gave their clauses extra weight. Bylaws - like administrative precedent - could always be challenged, if necessary in the London courts. Notoriously this happened over the often-cited right of Bath freemen to wield an absolute trading monopoly (except at market and fairs), which in 1765 was shown to have no legal authority and from then on proved unenforceable. Nevertheless the Corporation did enact many measures that it could and did enforce. Often drafted by the Town Clerk in consultation with senior officers or an *ad hoc* committee, these would be passed by vote at Council meetings and, when appropriate, publicised in handbills and press notices. Municipal legislation touched on many activities and in 1779 a committee was set up to examine all bylaws still in force. These included standing orders for Council business and internal accounting, and sundry regulations on the use of the hot baths (from times of bathing to appropriate dress), hours of market trading, and licensing of porters and basketwomen. The rules for sedan chairmen had to be formulated with special care since disputes were frequent - indeed the authorities had hurriedly to revise the tariff of fares in winter 1793-4 in the face of a chairmen's revolt. At different times the Mayor and Justices also promulgated specific orders concerned with keeping the peace, enforcing Acts of Parliament, and responding to royal proclamations. Examples include bans on street fireworks or the Shrovetide custom of 'throwing at cocks', restraints on hawkers and Sunday traders, and the seizure of indecent prints and seditious literature.

Cage see Lock-up and Guard House

Canal Companies

The river passage to Bristol had long been hindered by mill weirs, but efforts to win support for canalisation (meaning cheaper goods at Bath) repeatedly failed until the Corporation at last obtained a permissive Act of Parliament in 1712. Twelve years later, with progress blocked by commercial interests and perhaps lack of finance, the Corporation assigned all its rights to a company of 32 shareholders that included John Hobbs of Bristol and Ralph Allen of Bath - both looking to their future business prospects, one in timber, the other in Bath stone. The new company's engineering work, including half-a-dozen locks but no towpath, was completed in 1727 and the first laden barge passed from Hanham Mills upstream to Bath. A few months later Princess Amelia helped publicise the Avon Navigation with a boat trip to Bristol, and the c.£12,000 investment began to be recouped by tolls on goods transported - notably Bath freestone down to Bristol, and agricultural produce, building materials, pennant paving stone, and cheap coal (despite bitter opposition from local miners) up to the new quay at Bath bridge. Dividends were still modest and tolls much lower than the 5s. a ton then allowable, but the venture's overall success persuaded a new company, formed in 1733, to try extending the navigation as far as Chippenham.

Although this attempt failed, the idea of a canal link into Wiltshire (and beyond) was not forgotten, but it took until the 1790s for real progress to be made. This time the object was a brand-new canal, not further canalisation of the Avon. A committee under Charles Dundas, M.P. for Berkshire, raised substantial capital and in 1794 obtained a Kennet & Avon Canal Act authorising a large shareholding company and a 24-man executive committee. Technical and financial difficulties slowed progress but in 1799 the western section to Bath was finally cut after a new Act (1798) sanctioned an expensive realignment through Bathwick instead of having the canal debouch into the Avon at Bathampton. The committee had already decided against the engineer John Rennie's plan to continue the canal to Bristol and acquired a controlling interest in the Avon Navigation instead. The physical link between canal and river - via the Widcombe locks - proved much harder to achieve, needing another Act and another share issue. Barges could move from Sydney Wharf to Devizes by 1800, but only in 1810 did the first one pass through the whole Widcombe flight. After so much frustration for shareholders, the canal never did realise the attractive profits once envisaged. Its most immediate value for Bath was the link with the Somerset Coal Canal and the resulting fall in coal prices, but overall its economic impact never approached that of the original Avon Navigation which had given an enormous fillip to the growth of Georgian Bath.

Chamberlain

Use of the term 'Chamber' often implied not so much the Corporation as the city treasury. Over this the Chamberlain stood guardian. He was elected from among the Council members but, unlike the Mayor, Bailiffs and Constables, could serve spells of longer than one year. Between 1700 and 1793 two Chamberlains occupied the post for 4 years each, eight for 3 and seventeen for 2, providing helpful continuity but still no specialist expertise in handling accounts. The choice of H.E. Howse in 1794 from outside the Council's own ranks signalled the change to a permanently re-electable, salaried officer of Chamberlain-cum-Receiver, for which Howse received £200 a year and gave securities in a £2000 bond. The post was now analogous to that of Town Clerk, not least in being both part-time (Howse was also the government agent for stamp duties) and time-consuming. It was the job of the Chamberlain or his assistant to receive moneys due from rents, rates, and property renewals, which doubtless involved chivvying the collectors and harrying late payers. He likewise handled all loans, bequests, interest charges, disbursements on salaries, contractors' and suppliers' bills, freedom fees, Corporation gifts, tax payments, and sundry other items, either as agreed by the Council in advance or on his own initiative. The exact mechanics of the operation are not wholly clear, but plainly involved numerous transactions in cash, banknotes and bills of exchange, which the rise of local banking services only in part facilitated. There was apparently a four-key chest in the Guildhall, but the Chamber may also have kept coin and banknotes in other coffers. All income and expenditure had to be accounted for in statements to the Council backed up by bundles of tradesmen's vouchers (bills and receipts), and some years the books could only be balanced by taking out additional loans. A special Council committee sometimes audited the accounts. Chamberlains needed all the clerical assistance the Town Clerk's office could afford in drawing up the rent roll, handling payments, and transcribing the final accounts. Most were conscientious even to the extent of temporarily indebting themselves, and none could be accused of actual fraud (though in 1781-2 James Ferry may have come close). In 1731 the Council ordered its Chamberlain to produce bills quarterly before he authorised payments, and laid down too that no Chamberlain should become Mayor until his final accounts had passed muster, but that was to control spending and stop procrastination.

So much of the Chamberlain's work concerned land and water rentals and urban improvement projects, he inevitably assumed something of the role of city surveyor. Even with help from Council colleagues this was a burdensome responsibility, so that a separate City Surveyor's post was eventually created in 1765. The two offices reconnected in 1779 when the architect Thomas Baldwin added the brief of Deputy Chamberlain to his existing job of Surveyor. For a time the combination worked, but by 1790 Baldwin's increasing neglect of duty had become blatant and he was ordered to employ a clerk at the Chamberlain's office. In 1791-2, exasperated by his conduct and his failure to produce detailed accounts or to return rent books, the Corporation finally dispensed with his services and threatened to sue. The Corporation managed with the aid of a new clerk for only two more years before H. E. Howse became the first of the new-style Chamberlains in 1794.

••• See also **Banks**; **City Surveyor**; **Income and Expenditure**; **Rents, Rates and Taxes**.

Charities

Even the Corporation heart could melt at human need. Disbanded soldiers and seamen, civilian paupers, even on one occasion seven French prisoners, were occasionally relieved with small sums, and in 1774 the Council voted 50 guineas to victims of a serious fire at nearby Colerne. The elderly, impoverished Beau Nash received a similar 50 guineas for 25 copies of his non-existent *Memoirs* in 1755, and finally a city pension. Other gestures were less disinterested. Fear of food riots motivated the donations from the public purse in 1795 and 1800 to help supply the distressed poor with cheap provisions, and the bounties paid to recruits to the armed forces in wartime were less acts of charity than bribes to serve. The Corporation's powers of patronage also gave it some philanthropic leeway. Needy citizens could sometimes be found municipal jobs, especially the post of Pumper which had just such a charitable intent. Furthermore there were various bequests to administer - among them the Stirridge gift for Lenten bread (handed out at the Abbey Church), Queen Elizabeth's money towards fuel for Magdalen Hospital, and the Scudamore, Booth, Mohaire (or Moyer), Sherington and Taylor donations to the Bellott's, Lepers' and St Catherine's charities. Sir Thomas White's money, received every 23 years from the Chamberlain of Bristol, had a special use - to provide interest-free, ten-year loans of £25 to up to four local tradesmen at a time. It was no hardship to the Corporation, of course, to lend tacit support to other charitable fund-raising events such as sermons, subscriptions and concerts for the Bluecoats and Sunday Schools and the General Hospital. And private philanthropy and the voluntary charities they naturally approved.

••• See also **Almshouses**; **Infirmaries**; **Pumper**; **Voluntary Associations**.

Charters

The city's claim to be a corporate brorough rested on a series of royal charters dating back to Richard I's reign. All the mediaeval documents were superseded by an Elizabethan charter granted on 4 September 1590 which confirmed Bath's existing rights to self-governing status, gave it lordship over the dissolved Priory, and increased its area of jurisdiction well beyond the walls to the north by including a considerable tract of Walcot with Barton Farm. Except for a brief interlude from December 1684 when a charter of Charles II theoretically prevailed (and imposed a novel office of High Steward), the Corporation acted under Elizabeth's charter until 1794 when the document was finally surrendered and replaced by a new one. This largely re-stated its predecessor, but also increased the permitted number of city justices from two to nine, allowed for the appointment of a temporary Mayor or Recorder, and reinforced the Act of 1769 in placing part of Bathwick under city control. All the charters were essentially ring-fencing devices to exempt the municipality from the meddling (within defined areas) of Crown, Parliament, or the county of Somerset. Yet while they conferred valuable rights on its chief beneficiaries, i.e. members of the Corporation, charters seriously curtailed the rights of Bath's citizens at large who had no direct say in choosing their representatives, influencing the direction of municipal policy, or controlling the budget. In his famous cry for reform, *Rights of Man* (1791-2), Thomas Paine actually instanced Bath as a chartered monopoly that unfairly restricted the franchise to a 31-man Corporation oligarchy. He pointed out too that *local* charters damaged *national* freedoms - for Britons to work where they chose, for example. Having to purchase one's citizenship of a place (i.e. the city freedom) smacked, he thought, of feudalism.

••• See also **Acts of Parliament**; **Bylaws**; **Corporation**.

City Surveyor

Two 'Surveyors of the City Lands' existed by c.1750. These were fairly senior Council members whose function seems to have been helping the Chamberlain to collect rates and rents, superintend city properties, and produce plans and drawings for Council approval. The first Surveyor in the sense of City Architect - an outside appointment - was Richard Jones who accepted the post in 1765 at a yearly salary of £40. Though best known as Ralph Allen's clerk-of-works, Jones had immense experience of Bath buildings generally, and the Corporation's need of his practical advice arose over plans and contracts for the new Market and Guildhall - the largest redevelopment they had so far undertaken. In fact Jones's own design was not adopted and the scheme ran into difficulties anyway, leaving the Surveyor confined to routine maintenance (and perhaps valuation) of the Corporation estates. Jones moved into the better paid job of Sergeant-at-Arms in 1772, and in due course Councilman T.W. Atwood levered his protégé Thomas Baldwin into the Surveyor's post. Over the next dozen years Baldwin shouldered more and more tasks, not only redesigning and supervising the Guildhall project, remodelling the Cross Bath, and planning the new Private Baths, but elaborating the master scheme for the city centre that would be embodied in the Act of 1789. Furthermore, from 1779 he had taken on the brief of Deputy Chamberlain, a role probably not unlike that of the earlier Surveyors of the City Lands, but open to non-Council members and salaried. And all this on top of private commissions - culminating in William Pulteney's invitation to plan the new development of Bathwick. In 1790, already paid a double salary of £210 by the Corporation, Baldwin received the further appointment of Surveyor to the Improvement Commissioners at £200 per annum. The pressure was enormous and in 1791 the Corporation relieved him of his Deputy Chamberlain's post, perhaps already suspicious of his accounting for land and water rents collected. So tangled and perhaps corrupt did Baldwin's financial affairs henceforth become that he was stripped of his surveyorships to Corporation and Commissioners in June 1792 and June 1793 respectively. In both cases his successor was John Palmer, always Baldwin's rival but a better manager if a lesser architect. Palmer went on to complete the Pump Room, the Cross Bath, and all the other works in train. Baldwin's essential stamp on central Bath survived nevertheless, the only major public commission that evaded him being the Hot Bath, awarded to the younger John Wood just before Baldwin's reign began.

Commissioners

The Court of Requests and Bath Turnpike Trust were among the public bodies who entrusted their business to 'Commissioners', but in a local context the title referred most often to the Bath Commissioners (from 1766) and the Improvement Commissioners (from 1789) which are dealt with here.

Between 1700 and 1800 Bath changed out of all recognition, and the transmutation of a simple West Country spa into a sophisticated health and leisure resort, England's tenth largest city, was not accomplished without strains on its administration. Until 1766 the Corporation had largely coped alone, though the experiment of devolving paving, lighting and cleansing duties onto the parishes in 1757 can be viewed as one attempt to relieve a worsening load. The Bath Act of 1766 took delegation of responsibility a considerable step further by introducing - as several other towns already had - a quite new tier of local government, a board of Bath Commissioners, to oversee the whole outdoor environment, including street improvements, contractors' services, and the night watch. The Corporation did not wholly relinquish control, since, like each of the four parishes, it appointed four Commissioners (wealthy city creditors) to the 20-strong board, with the Mayor and the two J.P.s as members *ex officio*. Nonetheless the sixteen elected parish members easily outnumbered the Corporation nominees and did most of the work. Any male householder with over £50 in property and no financial interest in street services was qualified to serve.

Neatness, uniformity, and utility were the Bath Commissioners' watchwords as they set to work. Hanging shop signs were immediately banned in favour of flat signboards. Street lamps (now owned by the Commissioners) were increased in number, sometimes re-sited, and made to conform to set patterns. Inadequate pitching, uneven pavements, gratings, gutters, sewers, drainpipes, encroachments,

CITY of *BATH*, (to wit)

THE Commiffioners for Paving, Cleanfing, and Enlightening of the faid City of BATH, and the Liberties thereof, nominated and appointed by Force and Virtue of a certain Act of Parliament, made and paffed in the Sixth Year of the Reign of his prefent Majefty King GEORGE the Third, Do hereby give you Notice, within the Space of ten Days next enfuing the Date hereof, to *alter your Pavement & make the same in a line with Mr Atwoods/where altered to that of Mr Luishs thereofot & a half wide; also to take in the step now before your Door, & you are also desired to take in your Windows six Inches which are* belonging to, againſt, or before the Houfe or Land, now in your Poffeffion, fituate *in Cheat Street* within the faid City and Liberties, purfuant to the Directions of the faid Act of Parliament in that Cafe made and provided. And in default thereof, you will incur the Penalties in the faid Act of Parliament mentioned, for Recovery of which Penalties, legal Remedies will be purfued immediately after your Default. Dated this *17* Day of *Septr* 1783

By Order of the Commiffioners,

Smith

To Mr. Dunkerton

Clerk and Surveyor to the Commiffioners.

N. B. All Pitching and Paving to be under the Directions of the Commiffioners, or their Surveyor or Surveyors.

Order of 17 Sept 1783 from the Bath Commissioners to Mr Dunkerton requiring him to make his pavement 3¹/₂ feet wide in line with his neighbours, to take in his doorstep, and to reduce his shop bay window by six inches, all to be done within ten days.

obstructions (piles of dung or rubble, abandoned goods, unattended vehicles), obnoxious smells, and nuisances of many kinds were acted on, often by serving notices on the offenders and demanding action within three hours or ten days according to the offence - or in serious cases obtaining warrants through the courts. Enforcement was not always easy, and even penalising the contractors sometimes failed to improve the lighting and scavenging services that the public most complained of. Still, the Bath Commisssioners did a useful job (including numbering the streets in 1786), and every year opened their accounts to public inspection. When Outer Walcot obtained its Police Act in 1793 it was able to establish its own system of Commisssioners - though different from Bath's in demanding a higher property qualification, in empowering Commissioners to serve as justices, and in being self-perpetuating rather than elected. The Bathwick Act of 1801 provided for similar Commissioners.

A quite separate authority, the Bath Improvement Commissioners, came into being through the Act of 1789 for protecting the hot baths and springs, rebuilding the Pump Room, widening various streets, and creating five new ones. An earlier large rebuilding project, for the Guildhall and Market, had been supervised by a Council Committee and proved hugely controversial. What was envisaged in 1789 was more radical still and affected many more properties. Bath had not experienced a renewal project on this scale before - one that involved the valuation and compulsory purchase (or structural alteration) of so many buildings, compensation for owners and occupiers, the holding of jury inquiries, liaison with the Turnpike Commissioners, vetting of architects' plans, closure of streets, and all the detailed supervision of demolition and rebuilding. The creation of a statutory body of Improvement Commissioners - comprising 24 weighty local figures (including the two Bath M.P.s and owners of large estates) in addition to the whole city Council - provided a degree of independent (albeit still oligarchic) control that had been lacking in the Guildhall scheme. Corporation and Commissioners usually saw eye to eye, but the architect Baldwin's disgrace and dismissal caused delays, and there was dissension among the Commissioners themselves over the thorny issue of the *Bear* inn and the huge compensation demanded before Union Street could be built on this key site - a matter taken to Chancery and not settled for ten years.

••• For other Commissioners see under **Bathwick**; **Court of Requests**; **Turnpike Trusts**; **Walcot**.

Common see **Town Common**

Constables

Two (High or Chief) Constables were voted in annually to head the local peacekeeping force of Beadles, parish constables, night watchmen, and, in emergencies, sedan chairmen. This 'disagreeable Office' was the most junior post on the ladder of Corporation preferment and usually fell to recently elected Councilmen, though some did a second stint later in their Council career. Since no salary or perquisites came with the appointment, the Constables could expect to be rewarded within a couple of years by election to the lucrative sinecure of Bailiff. In theory their duties ranged widely: detention of suspects and wrongdoers, removal of beggars, suppression of riots and unlawful assemblies, maintenance of the constables' lock-up or guard-house (plus pillory, stocks and ducking stool), inspection of alehouses, and the collection of any specially levied taxes. In practice they must have worked closely with magistrates, Bailiffs, Beadles, and parish officers in a joint policing effort. Occasionally they risked being sued for taking unwarranted action (e.g. misusing their powers of arrest) but were always indemnified by the Corporation. As a symbol of office the Constables carried painted staves.

••• See also **Lock-up and Guard House**; **Police**. For petty constables see **Parish Administration**.

Coroner

As usual in corporate boroughs, the Mayor was also Coroner *ex officio*. He or his deputy consequently presided at Guildhall inquests, heard by a jury of at least a dozen, to establish the cause of any unexpected or suspicious deaths within the city boundaries. The Town Clerk would be on hand for legal advice as witnesses were called and the court probed the fatal circumstances - even the victim's possible state of mind if suicide seemed indicated. Actual *post mortem*s might have been rare, but other forensic evidence could be produced and nearly a third of Bath's 18th-century Mayor-Coroners had a useful medical background anyway. Sometimes graphic in their detail, records have survived from 1776 and reveal an average of just over four inquests a year. Accidents, suicides, and deaths from natural causes accounted for the bulk of cases, but murder (notably infanticide) also shows up among the verdicts. Easily the commonest site of sudden death was the river Avon (at least 170 drowned corpses were recovered 1744-1800), but people also died in workplace and traffic accidents; in fires and assaults; by ropes, guns and knives; befuddled with drink; or even 'disordered' by the full moon - the stigma of 'suicide' usually being avoided by some reference to mental imbalance. No other documents so well illuminate the personal tragedies and hardships of Bath's poorer classes at this time.

••• See also **Juries**.

Corporate Estates

Property meant wealth and was almost sacrosanct in law, so the fact
that the Corporation possessed land, buildings and other tangible
assets lent it extra authority and brought in considerable revenue.
Much of its real estate lay within the old walls. Here municipal
property made up about 80% of the area and included the lucrative hot
springs and baths. The Corporation owned the city walls themselves
and various scattered plots beyond, including certain parcels of land in
Walcot released for building from 1754 onwards (among them the sites
of Bladud's/Edgar/Prince's/Buildings, Milsom Street, and Paragon). It
held river rights within the Liberties and leased out the fisheries. It had
a plot at Haycombe. Furthest flung were its land-holdings at
Dunkerton and at Donhead St Mary near Shaftesbury, the latter in trust
for Bellott's Hospital. Almost all these properties generated income -
though in the case of the hundred or so sites granted by Edward VI to
support a grammar school and almshouse a vital question lay
unresolved, whether that income should be reserved for its original
purpose or subsumed, as in fact it was, in the city's general accounts
(the Chamber arguing that the specific properties could no longer be
identified). Profits from the Town Common due to the freemen were
another bone of contention, since the Corporation as steward of the
Common ultimately controlled what the annual dividends should be.

Unlike the Walcot and Bathwick estates, where lifehold tenancies
were gradually extinguished in favour of short-term leaseholds or
freeholds ready for development, Corporation properties continued to
be leased in the customary way, usually on three lives. Annual rents
stayed quite low under this system, but a heavy fine (i.e. fee) was
imposed whenever one of the three persons named on the lease died or
was otherwise replaced. By the 1770s the cost of such renewal fines
amounted to £100 or more on substantial properties, so that in some
years the income from fines exceeded the entire land rent roll. As an
alternative to life tenancy (typically of 99 years) the Corporation could
grant a shorter leasehold of 21 years (or a privileged 42 years for its
own members) not conditional on lives. Whichever arrangement was
preferred, the lease was properly documented and the city seal fixed to
the parchment. The Council's proprietorial attitude to its estate can be
seen in its requiring prior permission for building works and
encroachments (e.g. vaults dug in front of premises; doorways made
through the city walls), and then charging a nominal rent for such

concessions. Over the years quite large sums went on maintenance and renewal, which ranged from the upkeep of Bath Bridge or the farm buildings at Donhead St Mary to wholesale rebuilding of inner Bath during the 1770s and 1790s (which meant large payments in financial compensation). The commendable outcome, though, was a modernised city centre that in no way disgraced the Georgian splendours of the suburbs, especially considering the mediaeval street lay out and miscellaneous building stock that the Corporation had inherited.

••• See also **Baths and Pump Rooms; Guildhall; Income and Expenditure; Prisons (City); Private Estates; Rents, Rates and Taxes; Schools; Town Common; Water Supply.**

Corporation

The municipal reformers of 1835 found little good to say about the old Bath Corporation - an exclusive, privileged body that had robbed citizens of their ancient rights, misappropriated lands, defied the Chancery court, and reduced the freemen to a state of 'civic eunuchry'. From a purist, radical standpoint they were right. Self-elected, self-perpetuating, the Corporation clung fiercely to the levers of power. They alone set municipal policy, passed bylaws, obtained Acts of Parliament, elected the city M.P.s, chose the Recorder, nominated the Rector, ran the magistrates' courts, held the public purse strings, managed the town estate, regulated the market and hot springs, oversaw the Town Common, awarded major contracts, licensed premises, bestowed the city freedom. No matter that the Charter had been granted to Mayor, Aldermen *and Citizens*, the Corporation took every franchise to themselves and assumed the role of the borough's legal personality, symbolised by its monopoly of the city seal. Formally they comprised an annual Mayor, up to nine other Aldermen and twenty Councilmen, plus the Recorder, and from its membership provided the J.P.s, Chamberlain, Bailiffs and Constables who, like the Mayor, mostly served one year. It goes without saying they were all male. That there could ever be Councilwomen was a laughable thought.

This picture of unchecked patriarchy at once needs qualifying. For a start the Corporation's prerogatives stopped short at the Liberties. Immediately beyond the city boundary lay uncertain zones of

Detail from The Knights of Baythe, or The One-headed Corporation
*by 'William O'Garth' (1763), a satirical print that highlights Ralph Allen's
dominant political role on the City Council. Without fully consulting his
colleagues Allen had written to his old friend William Pitt, one of the Bath
M.P.s, describing the peace terms to end the Seven Years' War as 'adequate'.
Pitt, formerly War Minister, held the contrary view and took grave exception
to Allen's letter which he construed as a personal rebuke from his constituents.
In the complete caricature all the Corporation members but Allen are reduced
to mere ciphers identified by their occupational symbols - among them the
clockmaker Laurence, bookseller Leake, glazier Atwood, ironmonger Jones,
toyman and jeweller Davis, Town Clerk Clutterbuck, and saddler Chapman,
who all appear above. The resulting image has an almost surreal quality.*

negotiation and compromise with other authorities, the county administration and the large landowners. Bath justice too was circumscribed, and even the most trivial felony had to be tried in the county courts. The Corporation shared certain responsibilities with the parishes (e.g. for policing and Poor Law matters), with the Bath and Improvement Commissioners, and with independent bodies like the Turnpike Trustees and Hospital Governors. Over the suburban expansion of Bath and the spread of speculative building they wielded very little control. Their coercive powers in general were quite limited. They had no professional police. They feared mobs, riots, and violent confrontation. They could be lampooned. They might be sued. Their actions had to be geared to what public opinion would accept. So, in practice, checks and balances existed. Moreover, the Corporation's apparent scorn for democratic accountability looks somewhat different in the wider eighteenth-century context of political influence, favour and corruption. Bath in fact took pride in its independence. Thirty men sitting in private constituted the whole electorate, yes, but they were not wholly obliged to particular interests, they often secured national figures to represent the borough at Westminster, and by holding closed elections they at least reduced the risk that party strife might damage the spa's reputation for sociability and inclusiveness.

Routine day-to-day or emergency business was handled by an executive team of Mayor and magistrates, advised and aided as required by the other chief officers and the Town Clerk. The growing complexity of municipal affairs led to some devolution of responsibility (e.g. for city highways from 1766 to the Bath Commissioners), and the appointment of paid deputies or bureaucrats (notably to the Chamberlain's office) as a way of shoring up what was now an archaic structure. The City Council took the longer-term decisions and issued bylaws, yet here again much of the detailed investigation and drafting of proposals was devolved, this time to committees. What with regular calls to serve office (with penalties for unjustified refusal), Council meetings, committees, judicial duties, attendance at civic functions, and extramural business of all sorts, the Corporation élite lived busy lives. But of course there were compensations - the sense of status and power, the opportunities for social climbing and hobnobbing with the great and good (even with royalty if they were lucky), the chance to steer municipal policies for personal advantage, and - not to be cynically dismissed - the altruistic satisfactions of public service and civic virtue. To be on the Council was to be in the know, to be part of the club, to share in the dispensing of patronage, and to enjoy privileges and the paraphernalia of membership - civic processions and entertainments, a special pew in the Abbey, even (in 1728 and again in 1739) a place in the gallery of portraits hanging in the Guildhall. No wonder that a handful of dynastic families clung to their Corporation membership through two, three or more generations besides forging marriage and professional alliances with their colleagues. Ten Chapmans and seven Atwoods held positions on the Corporation during the eighteeenth century, and altogether a dozen families provided 52 of the members, including such familiar names as Bush, Collibee, Gibbs, Hicks and Woolmer. All the same, this was less than a third of those who served, and the conclusion must be drawn that the Corporation was in fact relatively open to fresh blood, especially to men of solid property and good connections - outstanding traits of the Cornish incomer Ralph Allen, for instance. Nor were Dissenters barred, providing they 'occasionally conformed', though several important Dissenting families (Marchants, Axfords, Evills, etc.) never had a seat at the Council table. A steady rise in gentility can be detected in the Corporation's make-up, as victuallers and common tradesmen gave way to professional men, polite retailers, and the odd esquires. Apothecaries, the commonest occupation represented, themselves gained status in the course of the century and were reinforced after 1750 by prominent physicians and surgeons.

••• See also **Charters**; **Council**; **Freemen**; **Guildhall**; **Higher Courts**; **Mayor**; **Parliament**; **Regalia and Symbols**.

Council

Best regarded as the Corporation in closed formal session, the Council had both legislative and executive powers. It could make and enforce bylaws. It could seek further powers by special Acts of Parliament or, in the rarest case, by requesting an amended Charter. And it had authority to exercise all corporate, customary and statutory rights within the Liberties. It was at the same time a narrow, self-elected, oligarchic body that decided matters in private and made public only what it wished. The Council alone chose who should be admitted to its ranks, who should serve as Mayor and magistrates, who as chief officers and lesser officials, and who should represent the borough in Parliament. This restricted franchise was contested in vain by the body of Freemen who claimed their rights had been usurped.

Six to twelve (very occasionally more) Council or 'Hall' meetings were held at the Guildhall each year - and always around the quarter days to deal with property matters and in September to elect the city officers, an event preceded by a reading of the Act for the Prevention of Bribery and Corruption. Officers were then sworn in ready for the mayoral year beginning in October. Notices and agenda of non-quarterly meetings would usually be sent out four days beforehand, separately copied out by hand and delivered by the trusted Beadles to Council members' houses. Members could be fined for non-attendance without good excuse, but on occasion meetings still had to be abandoned for lack of a quorum. The Mayor himself took the chair and the Town Clerk or his deputy made notes and wrote the minutes up later. A good deal of investigatory, monitoring, and drafting work was hived off to special committees of up to ten members. Inspection of properties, negotiations with owners, trawling through documents, auditing accounts, vetting bylaws, and preparation of parliamentary Bills often fell to *ad hoc* committees. More sustained committees and working parties were needed to supervise major projects such as rebuilding the Guildhall or the Hot Bath in the 1770s or to follow progress on lengthy court cases involving the Corporation. From c.1766 a virtually permanent standing committee seems to have watched over the city's water supply.

••• See also **Bylaws**; **Corporate Estates**; **Corporation**; **Councilmen**; **Elections**; **Income and Expenditure**.

Councilmen

The twenty Councilmen made up almost two-thirds of the Corporation membership, and from their ranks came the two Constables and two Bailiffs, chosen annually, and sometimes the Chamberlain. Vacancies for new Councilmen were filled as they occurred (through the promotion of senior Councilmen to the tier of Aldermen and through resignation or death) by the usual method of Council elections *in camera*. Potential candidates and their friends appear to have canvassed Corporation members privately in advance, and while family and other connections were strongly in a candidate's favour, his personal wealth, status, influence, and perhaps occupation, also counted. He had to be a freeman and - if not a practising Anglican - willing to qualify for office by 'occasional conformity' and to take the oaths of allegiance and supremacy. His need to be a resident was established in a King's Bench decision of 1741-2. A new Councilman paid no fees but seems customarily to have tipped the Town Clerk, Sergeants, Mayor's Beadles and Town Crier. Within a year or so he could expect to be appointed Constable and subsequently Bailiff, and he was eligible to serve on Council committees as required. Councilmen might nonetheless feel excluded from the real control centres of power. One complained in 1775 that too many Council actions were 'defended by darkness and secrecy' and that the renewal of leases, for example, was usually decided by a couple of members and then rubber-stamped. Oddly enough, nothing certain is known about a Councilman's official dress, but it is likely he wore a black gown.

County Administration

Bath's chartered status made it an enclave within Somerset, a privileged bailiwick in whose governance the Lord Lieutenant and County Sheriff had no right to interfere. By the same token its legal authority applied only to the Liberties, thus excluding Outer Walcot, most of Bathwick, and all Lyncombe and Widcombe, which nonetheless from c.1770 increasingly belonged to the urban, built-up area of Bath. These neighbouring parishes came under Somerset jurisdiction, or more specifically under the county division known as the hundred of Bathforum, administered by its own bench of magistrates. Where appropriate the city and the hundred co-operated, and until c.1720 Bath helped pay the Bathforum constable's wages. At times the two magistracies even acted as one. Thus in 1770, when two butchers returning home from market were attacked and robbed at Lambridge, it was a county J.P. (the architect John Wood II) who issued the arrest warrant and the Bath authorities who offered the reward. Both sets of J.P.s then examined the suspects jointly before committing them for trial. Policing the city's rural hinterland, where footpads, vagabonds, and even highwaymen might lurk, was no simple matter, but the failure of the county authorities to control the very suburbs of Bath undoubtedly caused some friction. Vagrants might be driven off the Bath streets but were 'suffered with impunity in the suburbs', ran one complaint in 1786. And why, it was asked in 1794, was nothing done about the notorious Holloway 'Rookery'?

The Bathforum magistrates met in Special Sessions and (from c.1788) extra Petty Sessions at certain inns in Lyncombe and Widcombe, until they were permitted in 1795 to use the Guildhall. Their deliberations were normally quite independent, but they covered much the same ground as the Bath Quarter Sessions and very likely employed a Justices' Clerk paralleling Bath's Town Clerk. Somerset held specific authority over Bath in two important areas. One concerned the Lord Lieutenant's right to levy a body of county militia from Bath, a right mainly exercised in wartime. The other lay in the county courts. Serious offences committed within the Liberties could be tried only at the Somerset Assizes or Quarter Sessions, and remand prisoners and convicts were held at the county gaols. As a consolation the city escaped having to pay towards the costs of county justice until a special rate was eventually charged with effect from 1820.

••• See also **Liberties**; **Militias and Volunteers**; **Prisons (County)**; **Somerset Assizes and Sessions**.

Court Leet

Every October - no longer twice a year as laid down in the Charter - Bath held a 'Court Leet and View of Frankpledge', a relic of its old manorial status and as a rule presided over by the Town Clerk in his guise of steward of the manor, though earlier in the century the Mayor judged cases himself and parish constables attended. It was juried, and appears to have inquired into boundary intrusions, rights of way, water diversions, health hazards, common nuisances and the like, but its proceedings were rather a formality now that its main functions had been usurped by the local Quarter Sessions. In 1776 the Corporation rather patronisingly informed the new Town Clerk, John Jefferys, that his stewardship of the Court Leet depended on his conduct there.

Court of Piedpoudre or Piepowder

Seemingly defunct by 1700, this was a Bailiffs' court, granted under the Charter to deal summarily with complaints regarding the market or the fairs - for instance about illegal trading, unfair tolls, or poor-quality produce. In 1703 one of the Queen's Household tried to compel the Bailiffs to hold a court session, with a 24-man jury, at the *Bear*, but the

Corporation resisted, presumably on the grounds that they alone could initiate proceedings. No other record of this court has survived. Any infringements of the market rules or breaches of the peace that the Bailiffs failed to settle were handled by the Court of Quarter Sessions, as were cases of profiteering.

Court of Quarter Sessions

Not to be confused with the *county* Sessions (held at Wells, Taunton or Bridgwater), this was a *borough* Court handling various administrative and criminal business. Capable of trying misdemeanours committed within the Liberties but no felonies whatsoever, it supposedly sat four times a year in the weeks following quarter days (Lady Day, Midsummer, Michaelmas, Christmas). It was presided over by the Mayor and Justices in the presence of the Bailiffs, Constables, Town Clerk (who kept a record of the proceedings), parish constables, and a sworn jury of between 12 and 24 citizens under a foreman. Sessions took two forms. Grand Juries heard presentments for civil actions, inquired into criminal charges, and decided whether to throw out indictments (with a formal 'ignoramus') or to proceed. Petty Juries tried cases and pronounced verdicts. Despite its name the Court frequently sat much oftener than quarterly in so-called 'adjourned sessions' to deal with straightforward administrative matters such as varying the terms of indentures (especially the binding of apprentices to new masters), making bastardy orders (regarding the custody of illegitimate children and payment for their upkeep), setting bread prices, reviewing turnpike tolls, and licensing victuallers. Other routine business included the the witnessing of oaths (taken by officials, juries, and - in 1778 - all Catholics resident in Bath), confirming the appointment of surveyors and rate collectors, and - most commonly in the 1750s - 'presenting' complaints on street repairs, obstructions and other nuisances. The magistrates also used the Court to make public orders, to issue warrants (e.g. for whipping beggars or searching premises), and to receive information which juries could then urge action on.

Hearings for misdemeanours covered cases of brawling, drunken or insulting behaviour, physical assault, vandalism, running brothels or illicit gaming houses, selling rotten meat or unlicensed goods, keeping insanitary slaughterhouses, regrating the market, and trading unlawfully in general. Those standing trial might be unbailed prisoners on remand brought directly from gaol, but the majority of defendants, plaintiffs and witnesses had been bound over to appear on a set day. Most surviving trial reports contain only the barest details, and we catch only rare glimpses of actual court proceedings - the summoning of juries, testimony of witnesses, payment of counsel, and so on. We do hear, though, of Thomas Sinnot's commital to prison on refusing to pay a 40-shilling fine for a gaming house (1713), of the lenient reduction of Elizabeth Wade's fine for assault once she pleaded guilty (1738), and of a butcher hauled off to prison for insulting the court (1779). In 1772 we catch the testimony of the young artist Ozias Humphry about his absconded master, and in 1794 discover the Crown prosecution briefs in several gagging actions against sedition during which the juries were virtually coerced into doing their patriotic duty of finding the accused guilty. Acquittals were common enough however (often 'for want of prosecution'), and sentences typically ranged from straight fines to spells of up to twelve months in Bath Prison, occasionally with hard labour. Litigants were sometimes ordered to pay costs and might be bound over on bail for good behaviour in future. Any criminal offences and civil disputes not within the Court's scope were committed to the county Sessions and Assizes or removed by writ of *certiorari* to metropolitan courts. The long-standing grievance that even minor felonies (such as petty larceny) could not be tried at Bath lingered on until the city at last obtained a more powerful Quarter Sessions Court in 1837.

••• See also **Assize of Bread**; **Higher Courts**; **Juries**; **Justices of the Peace**; **Licensing**; **Somerset Assizes and Sessions**.

Court of Record

This was one of Bath's oldest tribunals, held in theory every Monday at the Guildhall before the Mayor, the two Justices and the Town Clerk (or the Mayor and any one of the other three). As laid down by Charter, the two Sergeants-at-Arms took a prominent part in their capacity of attorneys - meaning, it seems, not so much real advocates, for they were hardly versed in law, as legal friends or representatives. Litigants could also employ their own counsel if they wished. The Recorder - witness his title - might also sit in this Court, and Lord Camden for one did so, but very exceptionally, in October 1769. Full hearings were held before a jury. In one instance - a case of 1727 brought by a tailor against Lady Dorothy Hesilrige for non-payment of a £4 debt - the jury foreman, a poulterer by trade, was reported as being remarkable for his blunders. The Court's main business was in just such personal actions to recover debt or claim damages (for trespass, breach of covenant, etc.) amounting to 40 shillings or more. Its jurisdiction was, however, limited to causes arising within the borough, and no defendant or witness could be pursued beyond the Liberties - though the summons could be posted on their Bath door. Proceedings sometimes dragged on for months as the Court entered pleas, served writs of inquiry, took depositions, remanded, awarded bail, and even adjourned for a period, before finally delivering judgment. Such delays, together with the fees plaintiffs had to pay the Bailiffs, Sergeants and others, must have been a disincentive to suing for small-to-moderate sums, which in turn prompted the setting up of the Court of Requests in 1766 to deal with ordinary trade debts. This meant that in later years the Court of Record, lacking business, would fail to sit for weeks or months at a time.

Court of Requests

Unmentioned in the Charter, this was a 'court of conscience' first authorised by the Bath Act of 1766 to simplify the recovery of ordinary (not gambling or matrimonial) debts under £2 within the jurisdiction of the Liberties. It sat on Tuesdays and occasionally dealt with other breaches of contract, e.g. a case in 1771 of a miswritten signboard. In addition to the whole body of the Corporation, the Act named fifty local tradesmen as Court Commissioners, four of them to sit by rotation with two aldermen each week to judge cases, award costs, and determine if necessary the rate per week or the period for debt repayment. It was a prompt if peremptory means of redress since common law procedures were set aside, litigants not legally represented, and fees kept low. On the other hand the Court could not demand seizure of money, bills of exchange, bonds or other securities, with the result that creditors often pressed for imprisonment - of 20 days for debts up to 20s., and 40 days for debts up to 40s. The threat alone might be enough to bring the parties to agreement without the case being heard. An effective agency in its early years, the Court had ossified by 1792 when a mere 13 of the originally named Commissioners survived and intervals between sessions had stretched to six weeks or more. The long delays forced some plaintiffs to turn to the more expensive county courts - where a summons alone cost 5s. as compared with 1s.3d. in the Court of Requests. Public criticism did produce extra Commissioners, but a thorough overhaul had to wait until 1805 when the Court's jurisdiction was statutorily extended to cover 35 local parishes and to cases of debt up to £10. The expanded workload (c.80 cases per day by the 1820s) then required the services of an expert barrister and an auxiliary bench drawn by rota from a much enlarged panel of 140-180 Commissioners.

Courts of Law see Coroner; Court Leet; Court of Piedpoudre; Court of Quarter Sessions; Court of Record; Court of Requests; Higher Courts; Justices of the Peace; Somerset Assizes and Sessions

Crime

'Security has ever been the distinguishing characteristic of Bath', ran one soothing refrain in 1763. But a place of such constant traffic, glittering with worldly goods, full of moneyed visitors, presented tempting opportunities nonetheless. Thieves, pickpockets and con men preyed on the unwary. Sharpers bound for Bristol Fair tried their luck at Bath. Criminal bands operated in both districts alongside receivers of stolen goods - the Poulter-Baxter gang in the 1750s, for instance, or the 'knot' of young delinquents reportedly working for silver coiners c.1792-4. Among favourite targets were the city's well-stocked retail shops. Haberdashers, drapers, toymen and watchmakers were particularly at risk of being pilfered or broken into. In 1770 one Widcombe tradesman lost over seventy watches in a single raid. Ordinary householders had goods stolen out of their 'areas' and were always vulnerable to opportunist servants, workmen and callers. On one occasion the culprits were boy chimneysweeps, caught with silver spoons. During a spate of vandalism in the 1780s and 1790s brass handles were wrenched off doors, iron railings and window bars taken, coal cellar grates removed, street lamps broken, sedan chairs slashed, ornamental trees spoiled. Boats tied up on the Avon in 1788 were damaged and sunk by large stones, and in 1799 the lion and bear statues that guarded Bath Bridge likewise ended up on the river bed. The persistent robbery of gardens, orchards and summerhouses prompted the setting up of a Gardeners' Society to tackle the issue.

Like the Guardian Society (for bringing offenders to trial) this was a private initiative.

Property crime of any sort automatically went before the county courts, as did serious crimes of violence. The evidence suggests that cases of physical assault, fighting, brawling and beating (heard by Bath's own justices) were common enough, but that heinous crime - except for infanticide - remained fairly rare. John Poulter (alias Baxter) remains the best-documented local criminal thanks to his candid confessions and the reports of his trial, imprisonment, last-minute escape, and execution at Ilchester in 1754. Several murderers, too, achieved a grim notoriety. Richard Biggs, convicted at Wells on his son's testimony for killing his wife, was publicly hanged in 1749 at Odd Down - his corpse, still in irons, washing up in the river at Twerton soon after. The following year the body of Richard Merrick, murderer of a pregnant girl in Walcot, could be seen exposed on a gibbet four miles north of Bath at Tog Hill. One of the Gordon Rioters, John Butler, died on the gallows at Bath itself in September 1780, watched by a great throng of spectators under the eye of a detachment of troops in the Corporation's pay.

••• See also **Courts of Law**; **Police**; **Social Problems**.

Diocese of Bath and Wells

The diocese impinged on Bath mainly through its Archdeacon, the Bishop's representative. The Bishops themselves were remote and unremarkable figures, often absent from the palace at Wells for long periods. All except Kidder were translated to Bath and Wells from Welsh sees and never achieved higher preferment. The benevolent Hooper was the most liked. Wynne spent much time on his Flintshire estate. Willes held office at Court as the King's 'decipherer'. Moss grew seriously rich from church revenues. It was he the Town Clerk saw in 1799 over the Rector's claim on certain Bath properties. The Archdeacon and the Rector of Bath were usually one and the same person.

••• See also **Rector of Bath**.

••• **List of Bishops 1700-1800**: *Richard Kidder 1691-1703; George Hooper 1704-27; John Wynne 1727-43; Edward Willes 1743-73; Charles Moss 1774-1802.*

Ducking Stool, Pillory and Stocks

These were not wholly redundant. Parish constables ducked one woman c.1705 and another, Joan Fletcher, c.1717 at the Mayor's behest. The stool was refixed c.1726, and the contraption still stood by the river on Boatstall Quay in the 1740s. The scaffolded pillory and the stocks must have remained in the Marketplace much later, since they were statutory punishments (e.g. for kidnapping and sex offences) until 1816. The last known use of the Bath pillory, however, was in January 1727 to punish Lewis and his wife, pimps and brothel-keepers, whom the crowd 'pelted severely'. In 1763 a Bath apprentice on a charge of raping two young girls was found guilty by the Assizes of assault and sentenced to 18 months in gaol - an initial order to stand in the pillory having been countermanded because of the popular retribution he might face.

Elections

The Council resolved most issues, including the election of individuals to office, by a vote (sometimes using voting papers), and then recorded the tally in its minute book. Appointment and re-appointment of officials (Sergeants-at-Arms, Abbey Organist, etc.) were usually routine matters, though contests did occur over some vacancies and over sinecures like the Pumper's. In theory annual elections for Council office took place at the pre-Michaelmas meeting when the names of the Mayor, J.P.s, Chamberlain, Bailiffs and Constables were decided for the ensuing Corporation year. In practice availability and the next-in-turn principle dictated choice, and penalties existed for refusal to serve without good reason. Even elevation to the rank of Alderman probably went by seniority and caused little argument. But the poll for a Councilman to fill a vacancy was a more serious matter, since every entrant to the select body of thirty affected the balance of the Corporation, politically and otherwise, for years to come until his eventual resignation or death. Occasionally an election result was contested. In 1742, for example, the apparently defeated John Taylor became Councilman after all, having legally overturned the original choice of Charles Biggs on the grounds that Biggs had not been a Bath resident on the election date. This affair led to a fresh bylaw clarifying the rules for Council elections, including a resolution that, if there were more than two candidates, the poll would be decided by simple majority on a single round of voting. This was a departure from the past practice in three-cornered contests of proceeding to a second round with just two contenders. It is clear that votes could be swayed by prior canvassing and that candidates' friends exerted their influence. Thus in 1758 the new Recorder, Thomas Potter, asked his ally the elder Pitt, now M.P. for Bath, to help elect onto the Council another Chapman, a nephew of Alderman William Chapman, to strengthen their interest. In the event the expected vacancy never occurred because Roger Hereford, then one of the Bailiffs but thought to be 'dying', lived for another sixteen years. The actor David Garrick, though a novice at Bath politics, had more success with his candidate for Councilman, John Palmer, in 1775, but then Palmer also enjoyed the powerful backing of the current Recorder, Lord Chancellor Camden.

Polling for Members of Parliament took place at a special meeting of Council when the Mayor, as returning officer, declared on oath that he had accepted no bribes or promises of reward. Only at these parliamentary elections did Council members' precise choices get recorded, a rare clue to party allegiance. Votes were often sewn up in advance, however, so that the election itself became an anticlimax. Wade could count on a Bath seat a good eighteen months before the poll in 1722, just as in 1790 it was so much a foregone conclusion that Pratt and Thynne would win that two other candidates simply opted out of the race. But there *were* exceptions - like the by-election of 1756 caused by the promotion of the sitting M.P., Robert Henley, to Attorney-General. Supporters of Joseph Langton of Newton Park expected to oust him, but at the last moment six of them went over to Henley and another twelve, in disgust at this desertion, stayed away. The Mayor, himself a Langtonite, declined to vote and unprecedently refused to hold the customary election supper. Sometimes victory could be overwhelming (Wade in 1734 took all 30 votes, and Pitt in 1757, with two absentees, 28), yet several contests were closely fought. Ligonier beat Langton 15 to 14 in 1748 despite protests that, not being a Bath freeman, he had no right to stand. Smith won by the same margin in 1766, only for the result to be challenged in the courts on the grounds that one of Smith's voters, a Dissenter, had not qualified himself to participate. Although the candidates at Bath's ostensibly clean, if very restrictive, elections may not have resorted to bribery *per se*, they still incurred obligations. Richard Pepper Arden, one of the city Members in the 1790s, appealed for help from Pitt himself to secure his constituency by means of favours to prominent local families, and he later requested a government post, no less, for Alderman William Anderdon. 'I almost begin to regret', he excused himself, 'that I have a seat which forces me to be troublesome'.

•••   See also **Council; Members of Parliament.**

Estates see **Corporate Estates; Private Estates; Town Common**

Fairs

Ratified by the Charter and managed profitably by the Bailiffs in the same way as the market, the Bath fairs took place twice a year - the 'orange fair' formerly on 3 February but after the calendar change (1752) on 14 February, the 'cherry fair' on 29 June and then 10 July. The dates carefully avoided clashes with other local fairs (Holloway in May, Lansdown in August, the new Kingsdown Fair in September), but the borough's own fairs suffered a much worse decline. As late as the 1770s they were said to feature 'sheep, pigs, horses, etc. and all sorts of merchandise', but the show of livestock was already much reduced. Around 1800 the Bath fairs were being called mere 'shadows' of what they once were, damaged by more regular beast sales, abundant retail outlets, and the cramped, traffic-ridden Marketplace site where the fairs were held. Gone by then were the animals and much of the produce, gone too much of the attendant revelry, leaving only a row of booths selling assorted fancy goods, haberdashery, and other cheap merchandise. Yet somehow the Bath fairs survived, still profitable enough in 1815 for the Bailiffs to award this perquisite to the Gaoler in part recompense for his loss of prison fees.

Fire Control

Being largely stone-built, Bath was more fire-proof than many other towns, but its cluttered central streets still contained timber-framed structures or housed trades dependent on ovens, kilns and open fires. In 1726 one particularly destructive blaze engulfed a block of old thatched houses in Horse [later Southgate] Street, and throughout the century fires broke out intermittently in workshops, stables, breweries and

other inner-city premises. By contrast the new Georgian planning
seemed altogether safer. Here streets were broader, hazardous trades
were often banned, and construction was in local stone with brick
chimney flues and tiled roofs. Yet just as many conflagrations occurred
in these modern developments as in the old districts. In 1747 it was
only the fortunate wind direction that saved the whole north range of
Queen Square from going up in flames. Later fires in South Parade,
Milsom Street, Avon Street and elsewhere resulted in serious losses of
property and sometimes in deaths. With their coal fires, illumination
by candles, and inflammable hangings, eighteenth-century interiors
could be dangerous environments. Sporadic threats of arson were
taken seriously but rarely carried out, the worst case being the
deliberate burning down of Williams's brewery on the Quay in 1800.

To reduce fire risk the authorities relied mainly on the vigilance of
the night watch and a rudimentary fire-fighting service. The city had
been donated a fire engine in 1694 and by 1713 seems to have had at
least two, equipped no doubt with leather pipes, squirts, buckets and
ladders. Some such appliance was used in 1746 to direct water from
the nearby baths onto a fire at Abbey Church House where Princess
Caroline was staying. This incident and the Queen Square fire a year
later led the city and individual parishes to improve their equipment.
In due course the Corporation had three engines stationed in the north
transept of the Abbey Church and inserted 'fire plugs' (hydrants) into
the municipal water supply for emergency use. The first locally-run
fire insurance company, the Bath Fire Office (1767) owned no engines
of its own to start with, but instead offered rewards to the first city or
parish appliances to arrive on the scene. A fire at Westgate Buildings
in 1779, though soon brought under control by five engines, at last
prompted the company to form its own brigade and to keep equipment
in readiness at Trim Street - and later at a 'Fire Engine house' in
Orange Grove as well. The rival Bath Sun Fire Office, established in
1777, also invested in apparatus. But fire-fighting capacity still failed
to keep pace with the rapid expansion of suburban Bath, as a
destructive blaze at half-built Marlborough Buildings only showed. A
fire in 1792 at Westgate Buildings was soon extinguished, but other
outbreaks in Borough Walls in 1791 and at the house of the master-of-
ceremonies, James King, in 1800 revealed equipment out of repair, a
lack of fire buckets, inadequate hosepipes, and poorly drilled
operators. Greater professionalism came with the merging of the two

Bath fire offices in 1806 and the creation of a fire station on Lower Borough Walls, but the chief responsibility for fire control remained with the insurance companies, not the city authorities, down to 1891.

••• See also **Insurance**.

Freemasons

The ostentatious display of masonic symbols carved into the Circus frieze might suggest a powerful organisation operating behind the scenes at Bath, but signs of real clandestine influence are hard to discern and even the ordinary practice of favouring brother freemasons in business can only be presumed. Freemasonry professed enlightened ideals of brotherly love, but this was expressed principally by bonding within the lodge and in charity aid to fellow masons. Minutes of Bath lodges dwell little on what was discussed (or drunk, for that matter) at meetings, but do report on balloting for and 'making' new masons and on their subsequent progression through degrees and offices up to the stage of Master. The core membership consisted of solid commercial and professional men, among them prominent shopkeepers, master craftsmen, innkeepers, attorneys, printers, medical men, a few clergy, and the odd artist or architect. Inevitably members and employees of the Corporation ranked among them. A number of landowning gentry also belonged, and masons visiting Bath from other lodges were always welcome. Similarly, Bath masons attended lodges elsewhere, and after the establishment of the Provincial Grand Lodge of Somersetshire took a prominent part in this too. Indeed John Smith of Combe Hay, one of the city M.P.s, became its first Grandmaster.

Freemasonry spread early to Bath. Its first lodge, inaugurated at the *Queen's Head* in 1723, was also the first provincial affiliate of the Grand Union, the umbrella organisation in London. Its full membership is not known, but Beau Nash - along with Viscount Cobham and Lord Hervey - was admitted in May 1724 during a visit to Bath by a leading light of the Grand Union, the scientist J.T. Desaguliers. This lodge soon expired and was erased from the national list in 1736. Four years previously a lodge with greater staying power had started meeting at the *Bear* where some of the former *Queen's Head* brethren joined it. Initially no.113 in countrywide seniority, it had risen to no.39 by 1786 when it finally merged its identity with the Royal Cumberland Lodge - a recent upstart but one named after

Britain's top freemason, the Duke of Cumberland, and sponsored by Thomas Dunckerley, provincial Grandmaster of Somerset and Gloucestershire. On 27 December 1784, the day of their patron St John, Dunckerley had in fact presided at a most public exposure of local freemasonry when all the Somerset and Bristol lodges met at the spa, processed through the streets (aproned and with their jewels and regalia), heard a brother mason preach at the Abbey Church, and then dined sociably together. In addition to the *Bear* Lodge (which since 1767 had in fact met at the *White Hart* and various other inns) the established Bath participants in 1784 no doubt included the Lodge of Perfect Friendship (reborn in 1765 out of the lapsed *Shakespeare Head* lodge) and the *Queen's Head* (previously *Saddlers' Arms*) lodge founded in 1769. Another lodge started at the *Pelican* in 1771 had not survived.

There may have been chapters of the separate Royal Arch masons at Bath (Dunckerley was also that order's Grand Superintendant) and certainly other societies existed that had a masonic flavour, e.g. the Bath knot of the Friendly Brothers of St Patrick (c.1787) and the Bath lodge of the Druidical Society (which met in a specially decorated room at the *London Tavern* c.1789). Even the Friendly Societies - in their more artisan way - bore some affinity to the cosy, insignia-conscious, drinking clubs that many lodges became, and which seem altogether to have lacked the sinister anti-religious motivation that some opponents claimed. In fact they were considered inoffensive enough (with their royal affiliations) not to be affected even by the Seditious Societies Act (1799) as long as they submitted lists of members to the Quarter Sessions.

Freemen

Bath freemen felt hard done by - unfairly disenfranchised, lacking any effective voice in municipal affairs, their precious trading privileges constantly gnawed at by non-freemen from other places, and the Town Common (their very estate) under the Corporation's thumb. Even the once powerful freemen's craft guilds had shrunk by 1700 to a mere three companies, the Merchant Tailors, the Shoemakers, and the declining Weavers. Three times (1661, 1675 and 1705-6) they pressed Parliament with their claims to the vote, but always in vain, for the Committee of Privileges and Elections remained adamant that the thirty Corporation members alone had the right to choose the city's two M.P.s. It was true that these thirty were themselves freemen, as Councilmen and Aldermen had to be, so that the Corporation, however exclusive its operations, could not be called a really alien body. On the contrary, its interests normally ran parallel with the freemen's - witness their shared endeavour in stamping out 'illegal' trade (i.e. by interlopers and non-freemen) and the great resuscitation of the trade companies in the 1750s under the auspices of the Guildhall. But towards the end of the century, in the vexed matter of whether or not to build on the Town Common, the Corporation sided with Bath residents and dug in their heels against the freemen who stood to gain most from much improved dividends. In this the Corporation at least remained consistent, for in 1714 they had very nearly denied the freemen their dividends altogether by applying the Common's profits to the wider public benefit of the Avon navigation.

Freemen could be created in three ways (a fourth way, by special nomination of the Mayor, being abandoned in 1714). The most traditional was an apprentice's almost automatic promotion on serving out a full term to an existing freeman, paying only the cost of his certificate and seal. The other methods were by Corporation election, either on payment of a hefty fee or granted honorarily. Asked for his opinion c.1789, the Recorder could see no legal distinction between either sort of *trading* freemen, i.e. the 'ancient' (apprenticed) freeman or the 'chartered' (elected). Honorary freemen came into a different category, since election in their case was intended to be a mark of esteem and not a licence to trade or compete with others. All through the century Bath went on honouring royalty, gentry, M.P.s, national heroes, and others to whom it felt obliged, and in the most exalted cases presented the inscribed freedom in a gold or silver box. This was seldom contentious and the city basked in the credit gained. On the other hand, by creating new *trading* freemen who had avoided the apprenticeship system, the Corporation - in the view of the customary freemen - were virtually legalising interlopers. Not only that, the entry fees they paid (rising from 20 guineas by 1730 to £75 by 1800) went straight into the general kitty and not towards the freemen's fund which still had to be shared with every newcomer. The huge entry of chartered freemen in the 1750s was caused, and made more acceptable, by the revival of the trade companies and the firm intention to enforce their monopolies. The customary election procedure for

Bath City.

To the Freemen of the City of Bath.

WE, the Committee of the Freemen of this City, do hereby give you NOTICE, that in Purfuance of the Power given us by a very refpectable Body of the Freemen to call your Truftees to an Account ; We have inftituted a Suit in the High Court of Chancery againft the CORPORATION of BATH, not only for an Account of the Rents and Profits of the Commons, but alfo for the Money arifing from the Sale of Gravel and Lime Stone dug out of your Eftate without your Confent, and to Compel them to improve your Eftate, or give up their Truft, and for various other Purpofes.

And, We do alfo give you NOTICE not to receive any Money which the Corporation on that Account may offer or Attempt to pay you, as you will not be fafe in receiving the fame, 'till after the Corporation have given their anfwer to the Bill filed on your Behalf, and you fhall receive further public Notice from Us,

Dated November 10, 1791.

freemen was waived for a time and the city treasury gained substantially from their fees. Alas, the subsequent Glazby judgment destroyed the freemen's monopoly and left them with few other benefits than paltry income from the Common, as little as 14s. each in 1785. No wonder then their efforts to secure a better return by developing their estate, their angry suit against the Corporation, and their brave shows of perambulating the Common in the 1790s, blue and white wands in hand, ending with the cakes and ale bequeathed them by Samuel Purlewent, their late legal counsel. Their strength, though, had already more than halved to some 200, and fewer and fewer apprentices were up-and-coming.

••• See also **Master Tradesmen**; **Town Common**; **Trade Companies**.

Friendly Societies

Voluntary benefit clubs existed at Bath well before Parliament gave such organisations full constitutional backing in 1793. The United Bathonian Society (1749), the Old Bath Society (1755), and the Union Society (1764), all pre-dated the dissolution of the local trade companies (craft guilds) in 1765, and another seven were formed in the 1770s and 1780s. In procedures they somewhat resembled the trade companies, but they had no regulatory function and their membership often cut across trade demarcations. Their main goals were mutual financial support, fellowship, and workers' solidarity, but they steered well clear of militant trade-unionism. Members paid into a common insurance fund which could be called on in times of need and sickness, and typically they were obliged (on penalty of fines) to attend monthly club nights, join in the annual dinner, share the duties of office, visit sick members and mourn at their funerals. What Parliament noticed, at a time of spiralling poor rates, was that these respectable self-help societies offered an economic safety net that saved their members becoming a burden on the parish. The 1793 Act therefore safeguarded their legal position (and crucially the possession of their money boxes), only requiring the societies to standardise their rules and to register at the Quarter Sessions. The Bath printer William Gye was foremost in helping the societies toe the line and persuaded them to fine any of their members guilty of seditious talk a punitive 10s. 6d. The Mayor and Corporation signalled approval in 1794 by walking in procession with the (by then twelve) registered societies to a service at the Abbey Church. Henceforth the march of the Bath 'mechanics' became an annual Whitsuntide event, accompanied by bands of music, colourful with sashes and club banners, and ending after church with each society dispersing to a feast at its pub headquarters. In 1795 three new societies took part, bringing the total to over a thousand members, but the magistrates had no fear of trouble from the festivities. From their point of view the Friendly Societies could be relied on wholeheartedly at this politically sensitive juncture as bastions of working-class loyalism and stability.

••• See also **Journeymen**; **Trade Companies**.

Gaoler

Alternatively known as the Turnkey (until this latter title came to be applied to *deputy* prison officers), the Gaoler owed his employment to the two Bailiffs acting in their capacity of municipal Sheriffs. In order to protect the Bailiffs from any costs or damages incurred in running the Prison, the Gaoler had to provide them with a bond of indemnity, naming his guarantors, for the large sum of £1500. He also undertook legal responsibility for the Prison, to keep it 'wholesome, clean and in good order at all times', to hold the inmates securely but without 'any oppression, cruelty or hard usage', and to execute all writs and orders issued by the courts. In practice his position was that of a contractor who ran the Prison as a private concern under minimal supervision. Having no official salary, he made a living by charging inmates a tariff of fees laid down at Bath Quarter Sessions (typically for admission, for discharge, for warrants and certificates, and for privileges such as special accommodation, beds, or linen) as well as by stark economies over food and fuel and by casual extortion. He distributed charitable donations, controlled social visits, or held prisoners fettered (cheaper than extra turnkeys), all as he thought fit. It was not necessarily a lucrative job even so. John Fisher, the Gaoler appointed in 1778, had to be helped out financially by a public subscription and municipal donation in 1786, just three years after he had personally been obliged to offer a substantial reward for the recapture of an escaped prisoner. He was replaced in 1789 by Thomas Biggs, who in 1794 also suffered the trauma of a prison escape when five inmates ran off after two army deserters he was trying to lock up struck him, bundled him into a prison cell, and removed his keys. This may have precipitated his death and replacement by George Griffin. All Gaolers at the Grove Street site were male, but at least two women appear to have run the former St Mary's prison for a time, Elizabeth Cooper in the 1750s and Sarah Sherston(e) a decade later.

••• See also **Prisons (City).**

Grammar School see **Schools**

Guides see **Baths and Pump Rooms**

Guildhall

If any building symbolised the corporate authority of Bath it was the Guildhall, Town Hall or simply the Hall. This was the headquarters of the Mayor and magistrates, seat of the justice system, focus of local administration, meeting place of the Council and its committees, the point from which national and civic legislation was enforced. It also had many subsidiary functions. The town archive and regalia were housed here, though by 1700 little but the swords and a few firearms can have survived from the former armoury. From 1728 it displayed the collection of Corporation portraits as well as the recently excavated Roman head of Minerva. The Guildhall was deemed the nodal point of Bath from which distances to other places were measured. It was where the Mayor and aldermen gathered before processing to the Abbey, and where proclamations were made and public notices posted up. It hosted Corporation banquets and balls, concerts and entertainments, public meetings and debates. Beflagged and illuminated to mark coronations, wartime victories and other national events, it visibly proclaimed Bath's loyal attachment to King and Country.

As its name suggests, the Guildhall had always been linked to the regulation of trade. The once powerful guild companies had dwindled in significance by 1700 and no longer met there, but the continuing intimate association of Guildhall and market was expressed in their very proximity. The old Guildhall, built in 1626-7, not only stood in the market section of the High Street, it occupied a floor immediately above the open-sided market house itself from which it was reached by a stone stair. On market days the traders' stalls and baskets, besides filling the ground floor, spread out well beyond the building, obstructing traffic and creating mess. Increasingly old-fashioned in appearance (with its double gables, casement windows, and niches on the north front holding effigies of two symbolic kings, Coel and Edgar), the structure was modernised somewhat in 1718 through fashionable sash-windows and wainscotting, then more radically in 1724-5 by adding a quite discordant Classical extension on the south side which did at least provide more space on the upper floor, a parlour or office for the Town Clerk below, and an internal staircase. The fabric of the older part was nevertheless unsound. In 1747 it needed propping up. By 1760 its state was described as 'ruinous' and Ralph Allen offered £500 towards a replacement. Six years later it was leaning noticeably and soon had to be cramped to prevent the walls from spreading further.

The Bath Improvement Act of 1766 had envisaged relocating the market, and by implication the Guildhall, to a nearby site on the east side of the High Street despite the high cost of clearing existing buildings and compensating their owners. Improvements to the Stuart Guildhall in 1718 had been funded by private gift, but the foundation stone of its successor, laid in 1768, bore the words 'erected at the sole expence of the Chamber of this city' to repudiate any charge that influence over the Corporation could still be bought. All the same, personal interests were very much at stake in the construction. Three architects competed over the initial brief, which once more envisaged a twin-purpose building, a town hall surmounting a market house. Once Thomas Lightholer's design had been chosen, preliminary site works began but soon halted to allow negotiations over the purchase of earmarked properties and, a related factor, over access to the proposed new Pulteney Bridge. As it turned out there was a protracted seven-year delay - time that one influential Councillor, Thomas Warr Atwood, used to particular advantage. Already City Surveyor and Deputy Chamberlain (as well as master plumber, banker and property developer in his private capacity), Atwood gradually assumed chief responsibility for the whole Guildhall-cum-market project. Assisted by his gifted architect Thomas Baldwin he drew up fresh plans, and by 1775 work was in progress on shops and market buildings which were intended to wrap round three sides of what would now be a free-standing Guildhall. It was at this point that an alternative plan came forward from the architectural partnership of John Palmer and Thomas Jelly, who suggested displacing the Guildhall from the High Street to a site overlooking the river and using the valuable High Street frontage for high-rent commercial premises with the market laid out behind. This seemed to have financial benefits to Bath ratepayers and, while the Council continued to back Atwood's scheme, Palmer's alternative began to attract a vociferous lobby of supporters who mounted a fierce attack on Atwood for self-interest, profiteering at public expense, and making exaggerated claims for his own project - and indeed Atwood's claims were soon shown to be misleading by an independent assessor from Bristol. Despite the clamour and the accusation of Council favouritism, the tendering procedure went ahead. But then, by a perverse stroke of fate, Atwood met with a mortal accident during demolition of a building on the site. This disaster quelled further protest and left Baldwin to revise the plan in detail and, between late

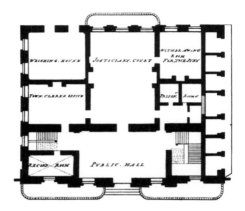

*Original plan by Atwood and Baldwin for the ground
floor of the new Guildhall showing the Town Clerk's Office,
Record Office, Magistrates' Court, Jury Room and Prison Cell.*

1775 and early 1777, to supervise construction. In the end decorating and furnishing were far from complete when the Corporation, eager to abandon the crumbling old Guildhall (unceremoniously auctioned off on Easter Monday 1777 and soon pulled down), occupied its grand new quarters. The finished building, a monument to civic pride, could even boast comparison with the finest gentry building in town, the Upper Assembly Rooms opened six years earlier. Nor was the magnificence any less when full-dress balls under a master of ceremonies began to be held for the town élite in the chandelier-lit banqueting room.

••• See also **Corporation**; **Council**; **Courts of Law**; **Market**.

Guilds see **Trade Companies**

Higher Courts

Confronted by challenges to its own authority the Corporation always responded with vigour. During the royal visit of 1703 the Queen's deputy Clerk of Market flung down just such a challenge by demanding the Bailiffs hold a Court of Piedpoudre over some question of the Bath market. The Mayor, William Chapman, spurned the order as 'contrary to the usual custom of Bath', was then sued by the Crown, and had to be defended next spring by his successor who carried the precious Charter up to London to demonstrate the infringement of local rights. Hardly was this resolved than the Corporation found itself embroiled in other actions. In 1705-6, with the aid of several citizen witnesses sent to Westminster, it managed to see off yet another bid by the freemen to widen the franchise, when Parliament's Committee of Privileges and Elections ruled that Council members alone could elect M.P.s. Rather more vexatious was the contest over Harrison's Assembly Room, built 1709, which questioned the city's ownership of the ancient walls. The new building stood immediately outside the walls but needed access through them onto Terrace Walk. Piqued by this upstart development, the Corporation not only refused permission but proceeded to build its wall higher, blocking the Assembly Room windows. Harrison's powerful backers then threatened to tear the wall down and the case went to the Court of Chancery - there to drag on expensively for another six years before petering out in some compromise. Meanwhile in 1712-13 another Chancery suit had been fought over the governance of St John's Hospital. It ended in 1717 with the award of the charity to the Master, leaving the Corporation with little but the right to appoint a new Master when a vacancy arose. Constant readiness to resort to the law can be seen again in the Council's decision in 1713 to join with other corporations in suing Bristol for payment of Sir Thomas White's charity due to 23 towns in rotation, or in the threat of 1751 to prosecute Somerset officials for executing warrants within the Liberties without sanction.

Several times the Corporation was itself in the dock, most embarrassingly in the entwined cases of St Michael's parish and the Grammar School which both concerned Tudor lands supposedly misappropriated by the city authorities. Out of 56 properties granted to Bath in 1585 St Michael's claimed title to 32 as properly due to the parish for the upkeep of the church and parish poor, whereas since 1646 the Corporation had merely assigned it the rents that the properties yielded. In September 1734 a Chancery Commission of Charitable Uses met at Bath to launch a jury inquiry into the affair, and for the next seven months the Mayor and Town Clerk were repeatedly called on to produce documentary evidence under pressure from the Lord Chancellor and threat of confinement in the Fleet prison. In May 1735 the Commission found the Corporation guilty, despite a stout defence, and required it to repair the crumbling parish church, but the

Corporation lodged objections and only later placated the parishioners by applying a 500-guinea donation from General Wade, its M.P., to rebuilding St Michael's completely. The Commissioners had meanwhile been looking into another grievance, namely that the Corporation had embezzled the income from the hundred odd properties originally reserved, under Edward VI's grant, for the support of the Grammar School and St Catherine's almshouse. Again found guilty, the city administration was fined £500 and told to locate the relevant properties within six months or suffer a £5000 penalty. None of this was in fact executed, but here too some amends were finally made when a brand new Grammar School opened in 1754. What no-one had bargained for was that the St Michael's cause would be resurrected in 1775 following a Corporation appeal. This time the Chancery proceedings took place in London and entailed great expense in hire of learned counsel, frequent attendance by the Town Clerk, and the belated discovery that many of the old deeds sent to London for transcription in the mid-1730s had since disappeared. The case was reinvestigated at length, argued twice in 1777 and 1787, reported in 1797, and judged at last in 1798 mainly in the Corporation's favour. It must have felt like a Pyrrhic victory given the inordinate costs of the affair. Compared with the St Michael's suit, most other actions in the higher courts seem quite small beer. Among them might be cited the King's Bench trial of 1742 regarding John Taylor's non-election to the Council, and three cases from the 1790s - over the freemen's demand to build on the Town Common, the Improvement Commissioners' need to demolish the *Bear* inn, and the claim of Walcot parish on the Huntingdon Chapel for payment of poor rates.

••• See also **Freemen; Somerset Assizes and Sessions**.

Hospitals see **Almshouses; Infirmaries**

Hundred of Bathforum see **County Administration**

Improvement Commissioners see **Commissioners**

Income and Expenditure

The volume of Chamberlain's business rose year on year. Between 1700-20 and 1780-1800 average annual turnover leapt tenfold from c.£700 to over £7000, with marked peaks whenever the Corporation embarked on a building campaign - as, for instance, around 1751-5 (Pump Room, King's Bath, Grammar School, Bath Bridge) and 1772-80 (Prison, Waterworks, Market, Guildhall, Hot Bath). The unusual expenditure in the 1750s was partly met by the fees from tradesmen taking up their city freedom, but this proved a one-off bonanza. Large undertakings generally had to be capitalised by borrowing, typically in the form of £100-£300 municipal bonds at fixed interest rates of $3^1/_2$-5%. Members, relations and friends of the Corporation all took advantage of such a secure investment and lent sums ranging from £100 to £4000. Gradually the Chamber's debt increased from around £5000 c.1730 to £10,000 in 1768, £25,000 in 1778, and over £31,000 by 1798 - quite a high level of financial exposure as well as costly (at over £1500 per annum by 1798) in servicing interest payments. But lenders were not deterred. Bonds issued under the city seal were far less risky than bank deposits or investments in turnpikes, canals, tontine shares, and the like.

Loans aside, there were three main sources of city income - quit rents (plus the substantial dues from the Bailiffs and Pumper), water rates, and 'fines' imposed for renewing life tenancies or granting freedoms. The receipts from city properties in rents and water charges grew steadily up to 1775 as Bath expanded, and then doubled again in the boom period that followed. Income from fines fluctuated year by year, but once the surge of new freemen in the early 1750s was over, renewals of lease made up the bulk of this revenue. The Chamberlain could tap several other sources, such as monthly receipts from the weighing engine (after 1763) and eventually the profits from the Hot Bath and New Private Baths, yet other potential funds by-passed the Chamber altogether, e.g. market rents and court fees which mostly went to the Bailiffs and Town Clerk. Nor were occasional handsome donations, such as the gifts of Bath M.P.s, available for general purposes since these, like charity income, came already earmarked. In the same way rent accruing from the Town Common properly belonged in the separate freemen's account.

Expenditure was far more miscellaneous. The category 'Stipends and Out Rents' covered some of the most predictable outgoings.

Certain officers and employees received salaries and allowances - notably the Mayor himself (towards his year's expenses), Recorder, Town Clerk, Chamberlain or Deputy Chamberlain (mainly to pay assistants), City Surveyor, Sergeants-at-Arms (from 1783), Beadles, Town Crier, Headmaster of the Grammar School, Abbey Organist, the City Waits, the water turncocks, and the Tompion clock keeper - a paybill that totalled almost £1000 by the 1790s. A few others (including Beau Nash in his final year) enjoyed a civic pension or annuity. Regular bequest payments went to Bellott's Hospital, St Catherine's, and other charities, and smaller sums to the beneficiaries of certain residual ground rents. Interest on loans was another predictable cost, but one that varied from year to year as new funds were raised and old loans liquidated. Rates, rents, taxes and insurance premiums also fluctuated, as did payments for services such as bellringing, sweeping Orange Grove, delivering coal and candles, making Beadles' coats, or inscribing the accounts. All kinds of administrative costs arose - stationery supplies, press notices, transport of paupers, expenses at the county courts, beer for juries and sundry workmen, corporate entertaining, fire engines, weighing machines, matting for the Pump Room, gold boxes in which to present honorary freedoms. The expense of obtaining Acts of Parliament or defending suits in the London courts was another drain on funds, especially serious from 1777 on account of the long-drawn-out case with St Michael's. By far the greatest outlay, though, was on maintaining and improving the city fabric, seen in countless small repair jobs and refurbishments as well as in successive projects to open up, rebuild and classicise the centre of Bath, beginning with the demolition of the North, South and West gates in the mid-1750s. What is easily overlooked in these renewal schemes is the considerable expense of preparing the sites before construction even started. For example, by 1768 the Corporation had already spent a tidy £11,000 in buying and demolishing properties on the east side of High Street for the future Guildhall-cum-Market (purchasing the old *White Lion* alone had cost nearly £1100) and there was more to come. These figures were substantial enough set against total annual income, but they were dwarfed by the financial commitments of the 1790s. No traditional loan arrangements could have raised the £83,000 (at a conservative estimate) needed for a scheme which involved creating new streets and widening/refronting others, besides rebuilding the Pump Room and making the New Private Baths. Half that sum, it was true, would be recouped from improved properties, and the Corporation could underwrite some of the rest, but that still left £25,000 to find through loans secured on the profits of increased turnpike tolls. The enabling Act of Parliament (1789) saddled the Chamber with repayment commitments stretching well into the next century. Financially compromised as it was, the Corporation can hardly have viewed the national credit crisis of 1793 and the ensuing war against France with much equanimity.

••• See also **Banks**; **Chamberlain**; **Charities**; **Corporate Estates**; **Rents, Rates and Taxes**.

Infirmaries

Better-off spa visitors could afford private lodgings, medicines and doctors. The poor who travelled to Bath for treatment could not, and it was for these that the first post-monastic infirmaries were built, notably Bellott's Hospital in Bell Tree Lane around 1609 and the General Hospital in 1738-42. Thomas Bellott's charity was a gift to the city, its philanthropic founder providing not only the site and building but endowing it with lands at Donhead St Mary, near Shaftesbury. Essentially it catered to 'lame pilgrims' who came for the cure on a magistrate's licence, and it qualifies as an embryonic infirmary because it provided for attendance by a surgeon and free access to the

hot springs, in theory for up to four weeks per patient. Originally it opened for a mere three months in the year, and in the eighteenth century still for no more than six, late March to September. The Scudamore bequest (1652) enabled a visiting physician to be appointed at a modest annual fee of £8 to certify admissions and advise patients. Despite the arrival of the General Hospital on the scene, Bellott's went on accepting patients up to a maximum of sixteen at any one time. The Corporation handled its accounts, maintained the premises, occasionally supplied bathing gowns and linen, and paid a nurse £2 a year and 2s.4d. for every patient in care. Thanks to the Mohaire (or Moyer) bequest, the city also supported the Lepers' Hospital, giving the nurse there an annual £2.10s. and the poor she accommodated in a 'hovel' beside the Lepers' Bath £10 (later £12.50s.), with occasional extra sums for shrouds and burials. How these patients were chosen among so many needy applicants is unclear.

By contrast, selection procedures for the General Hospital were trumpeted across the land. Ostensibly an independent, self-governing institution, it existed in almost symbiotic relationship with the Corporation. The city fathers had at first been wary of this unpredictable venture that seemed to impinge on their control of the hot springs. But though they prepared a counter-petition, they refrained in the end from opposing the Hospital Bill of 1738, aware that it laid down quite stringent rules for regulating admissions and returning patients to their parishes after treatment - including deposits of £3-£5 from each patient for their eventual travel home and their conveyance thirty miles beyond Bath by the Hospital beadles. These requirements provided a highly convenient excuse for refusing access to the baths to all but the *sponsored* poor and for regarding anyone unable to brandish a certificate as a vagrant. On this understanding the Corporation guardedly welcomed the Hospital while restricting its patients to treatment at the Hot Baths, the least fashionable of the bathing establishments. For some years following the Hospital's début in 1742, worries persisted on both sides that it might indeed be attracting beggars to the city, despite all the national publicity about the strict entry conditions that applied and the fact that powers to arrest vagrants (spelled out in the Hospital Act) reached to 'Walcot', 'Widcombe' and five miles round Bath. On the other hand the arrival of such a prestigious philanthropic institution undoubtedly shed an extra lustre on the spa's reputation. The influential Ralph Allen was one of its chief backers, as were many medical practitioners at Bath who saw in the Hospital prospects for personal advance. Allen was a governor from the start (and President in 1742-3) and the number of Council members on the Hospital board - besides the Mayor and J.P.s who had *ex officio* status - grew steadily. At the same time no amount of Corporation involvement could obscure the General Hospital's practical irrevelance to most Bathonians. Not only were the city's own sick poor barred from treatment there, but the better-off, if they thought of becoming subscribers, were denied the privilege - normal elsewhere - of recommending patients for beds. So instead of regular benefactions from local people it was the casual donations of visitors and the vital half-yearly church collections that in large part financed it.

Two smaller medical institutions *did* cater to the neglected poor of Bath as well as providing further career ladders to practitioners. The Casualty Hospital concentrated on accident victims and may have been the first in Britain so to specialise. A surge of accidents in the overstretched building trade coincided with the availability in Bath of an experienced Bristol-trained surgeon, James Norman, who opened his establishment at 38 Kingsmead Street in 1788. According to its rules it served Walcot alone, though urgent cases from other parishes, including people saved from drowning, arrived there for treatment too - since, unusually for its time, the Casualty Hospital imposed no admission charge. Funded by subscription and donation and managed by five trustees, it had 10-12 beds for serious cases, recorded a surprisingly high success rate, and between 1788 and 1796 cared for some 500 accident victims in-house and over 3000 more as out-patients.

The origins of the City Infirmary went back further. From 1747 the poor of Bath, Walcot and Bathwick (unless employed servants or already on parish relief) had been eligible for medicines and an apothecary's advice at a dispensary promoted by the Pauper Scheme. This was a charity primarily intended for working-class families who had migrated to Bath and, unable to claim poor relief, faced destitution if the breadwinner fell ill. In 1764 the scheme was extended to cover surgical needs, and in 1771 alone succoured over 3000 sick and injured - 'Poor Objects most of 'em in the greatest distress'. With funds running low the Pauper Charity made a fresh start in 1776. Subscribers were allowed to recommend deserving cases, a series of annual benefit concerts brought in further income, and the organisation struggled on until its transmutation into the City Infirmary and Dispensary in 1792. Anxious about containing infectious diseases, the committee fitted out the former Alfred Hotel on Lower Borough Walls with hospital wards, an out-patients' clinic, a dispensary (hitherto located in Wood Street), and quarters for a resident apothecary. Three Bath physicians gave daily consultations, vetted admissions (over 100 a year) and made home visits. Running up to 1800 the Infirmary treated three times as many out-patients as the Casualty Hospital, but though there was obvious scope for rationalisation between the two, their grand merger into Bath United Hospital was postponed for another quarter century.

Inquests see Coroner

Insurance

Fire was the chief insurable risk. People were rarely covered for other damage to property (e.g. from river floods) or for losses from crime, accidents and personal injury. By contrast Bathonians were paying fire insurance premiums even before 1720 on houses, licensed premises, workshops, merchandise, furnishings and utensils - though the small print on 18th-century policies tended to exclude claims on money and bills, jewellery, pictures, gunpowder, and losses incurred through enemy action or civil disturbance. The Corporation and its tenants originally took out policies from London firms such as the Sun and Royal Exchange. Not until 1767 did a local company set up, the Bath Fire Office, said to be the first founded in the provinces since 1720 and offering 3% more than London in the event of a claim. With sixty shareholders and twelve substantial local directors it commanded confidence, issuing 460 policies graded according to the risk involved during its first year of operation. In the later 1770s it opened branches in Bristol, Chippenham and Melksham, but on its home ground faced opposition from a rival, the Bath Sun Fire Office from 1777, the same year that the Corporation began to require all city properties to be insured as a condition of renewal of lease. Although the [Old] Bath Fire Office alone had issued around 5750 policies by the end of 1792, competition was intensifying as London firms like the Royal Exchange, Sun, and Phoenix installed their own agents at the spa. These did not, however, maintain fire engines and train men ready for emergencies - unlike the two Bath-based offices which joined forces in 1806 to make their fire-fighting role more efficient.

Fire insurance dominated but other types did exist. For example special militia offices sprang up during the American and French wars (1775-83 and 1793 onwards) to safeguard people from serving in the Somerset Militia. An insurance premium of a guinea entitled clients to ten guineas - more than enough to buy exemption should they be unlucky in the ballot. A different sort of cover was achieved by subscribing to the Society of Guardians' scheme which guaranteed that criminal offenders, if caught, would at least be brought to justice in the county courts.

••• See also **Fire Control**.

Journeymen

Around the age of twenty-one an apprentice completed his contracted term, a moment of happy release often marked by some workplace ritual. Unless he had the capital to risk setting up at once on his own or in partnership, he then became a journeyman, a skilled or semi-skilled employee working for others - typically on a fairly low wage that was standard throughout his trade in that locality. It was rarely enough to marry on. A journeyman in a genteel occupation might cut a brave figure, one contemporary noted, yet without other financial resources he would always find it a struggle to support a wife and family. Certain journeymen did manage to save enough to become self-employed, but many others never escaped their humble rank. Some lived a nomadic existence, moving on as the demand for hands fluctuated.

Income levels being so crucial to their prospects, it was natural that journeymen periodically agitated for better wages and conditions. Bristol weavers and Kingswood miners had given early lessons in industrial protest, but at Bath little was heard about 'combinations' - incipient trade unions - until the 1760s (specifically in 1760, 1763-64 and 1768) when the journeymen tailors collectively pressured their employers for more than 2s. a day by simply neglecting the houses of call (pubs like the *Crown* in Chapel Row, the *Apple Tree* in Stall Street) where they were hired and paid. In 1768 the master tailors resisted the demand 'so unwarrantedly imposed on them' for an extra 6d. per day for half the year, but the journeymen continued to organise and by 1774 had a union HQ at the *Coach & Horses*, Horse Street. Strike action in spring 1775 hit the tailoring trade across Bath and forced customers to send their orders to London. For a time the employers seemed to capitulate by offering their workmen 2s.6d. a day, but the rate soon returned to 2s. The increasing cost of living nevertheless emboldened other sectors, and in August 1776 the journeymen carpenters decided to strike for a wage increase of 3s. a week. Siding as always with the employers, the magistrates warned publicans not to allow meetings of 'associating Journeymen Carpenters, Taylors, or others' on pain of losing their licence, and (through the Town Clerk) promised their help in suppressing the conspiracy. Undeterred, the journeymen shoemakers attracted notice in 1777 by openly soliciting financial aid for their colleagues on strike at Bristol.

Employers could always break strikes by importing hands who were prepared to work for the old wage. In 1784 a group of frustrated journeymen (one armed with a pistol) resorted to violence against cut-price tailors, and there was similar bitterness over the use of scab labour during the shoemakers' and the staymakers' disputes of 1792, a year when local coal-miners also took strike action. The following year nine men came before the bench charged with conspiracy and combination, but even though the anti-sedition laws made association increasingly dangerous the shoemakers still downed tools in 1795, and the journeymen house-painters in 1796. Only the Combination Acts of 1799-1800 quelled the activists for a time, but by 1803-4 the shoemakers would again be organising for fairer pay, and this time with national support.

••• See also **Friendly Societies**; **Master Trademen**; **Trade Companies**.

Juries

Any resident Bath male aged 21 to 70 who owned land worth £10 per annum, or who (from 1730) leased property valued at £20 per annum, was eligible for *borough* but exempt from *county* jury service. Lists kept by parish constables would be available to Bailiffs and others responsible for furnishing the juries needed at proceedings of Bath Quarter Sessions, Court of Record, Court Leet, and Coroner's Inquests. Solid tradesmen 'paying scot and lot' made up the bulk of jurymen, with the same names cropping up repeatedly on lists of both juries and parish tithingmen - whom Quarter Sessions juries actually had to approve. They were sworn in ahead of court hearings and could then be fined for not appearing on the day. Though twenty four might be detailed, in practice any number from twelve to eighteen sufficed to decide verdicts. After hearing evidence they could also recommend judicial action on other matters such as suppressing public hazards and nuisances. Court Leet and Coroner's juries were sometimes treated afterwards to beer at Corporation expense, but any compensation for other forms of jury service must have come out of court fees.

Justices of the Peace

Until 1794 Bath justice was executed by an annually changing bench consisting of the current Mayor and two justices sworn in alongside him. (The Recorder, who was nominally a member *ex officio*, seldom if ever sat.) All three had to be Aldermen and one would always be the outgoing Mayor which ensured a measure of continuity. The new Charter of 1794 increased the number of elected J.P.s to between four and nine, and made Councilmen eligible for the first time. Responsible to the Crown, they acted either through the regular borough courts (Quarter Sessions and Court of Record) or at any other time in summary session when they could hear evidence, interpret the law, and take decisions, all without the participation of counsel or jury. The Mayor and both J.P.s presided at Quarter Sessions, but in summary proceedings often just one of them (or the Town Clerk alone for certain administrative matters). The summary case load grew steadily - to over 700 cases a year by 1776-7, around 850 by 1786-7, and over 1000 in 1793, heard on 266 of the 309 available weekdays of the year. Heading the list of routine matters came indictments for common assault and related breaches of the peace (at least a third of individual cases). Next in frequency came Poor Law affairs, followed by bailable writs (for recovery of debts), then cases of theft, vandalism, and other property offences, and finally various administrative business - licensing sedan chairs and alehouses, attesting soldiers, confirming appointments, and witnessing oath-taking. Relatively few cases proceeded to the Quarter Sessions and of those that did many were thrown out when plaintiffs failed to appear.

The Bath justices had powers to issue search and arrest warrants, dismiss charges or prosecute, make court orders, fine, demand bail and legal costs (on a set scale), and commit to gaol. Only with respect to felonies and other serious offences were their hands tied, for after preliminary examination they had no option but to refer these cases to the county courts and to remand the accused meanwhile in a county gaol. This was what happened in the case of Mrs Leigh-Perrot, Jane Austen's aunt, arrested in 1800 on suspicion of stealing lace, seen briefly by the Bath J.P.s, transported to Ilchester and held for long months there (in the gaoler's house), and finally tried - and exonerated - at Taunton Assizes. Pressure on the justices mounted in the later eighteenth century. The Gordon Riots of 1780, when mob violence briefly convulsed Bath, frightened the Corporation as much as anyone, and made the Bath and Bathforum J.P.s readier in future to close disorderly alehouses, outlaw boxing matches, suppress revels, fend off food riots with subsidised provisions, and clamp down on rabble-raising politicians. Quiet diplomacy might also quell trouble, as in 1789 when the magistrates stepped in to avert a duel. Otherwise public orders issued from the Guildhall in a steady stream - from calls on *émigrés* to produce their passes to reminders about bans on Sunday trading. Even the hour that old clothes men and sandboys could cry their wares through the streets was formally laid down (and informally disregarded). Yet for all their labours J.P.s, by law, were not remunerated. Nor is there any evidence that they profited, at least at Bath, from bribes and favours.

••• See also **Assize of Bread**; **Court of Quarter Sessions**; **Court of Record**; **Crime**; **Licensing**; **Mayor**.

Kingston Estate

Ownership of land at Bath went through some upheaval after the dissolution of the Priory in 1539, with the subsequent round of purchases, grants, consolidations, and legal settlements spreading over the next eighty years. The fate of the Priory estate that lay within the city walls was for it initially to pass into private hands, and then in 1572 to be divided when its landowner, Edmund Colthurst, presented the Abbey Church and adjoining litten (graveyard) to the Corporation while retaining the rest. For the century up to 1711 the private (and larger) portion belonged to the Hall family of Bradford-on-Avon, and after that to the aristocratic Kingstons who began its urban development. Graced by Terrace Walk and the Parades, lodging houses, two assembly rooms, theatres, good shops, and a popular coffee-house, the Kingston estate soon became a main focus of fashionable Bath. Since its boundaries (wholly within St James's parish) rubbed up against Corporation properties, there was of course ample scope for periodic minor confrontations between the two landowners, not least over water supplies, though the Corporation held most of the important cards. One institution, the private Abbey Baths (1766), must have irked the Corporation in particular. It intruded on their dearly held monopoly over hot-water bathing and, with nearly 800 clients in 1771, was certainly deflecting custom from the city establishments. The effort that soon went in to rebuilding and gentrifying the Hot Bath shows the Corporation's determination to regain the initiative from the Kingston upstart.

••• See also **Private Estates**; **Water Supply**.

••• **List of Lords of Kingston Estate**: *John Hall to 1711; Rachel (Bayntun) Pierrepont, Countess of Kingston 1711-22; Evelyn Pierrepont, 2nd Duke of Kingston (this title from 1726) 1722-73; Elizabeth Chudleigh, self-styled Duchess of Kingston 1773-88; Charles Me(a)dows Pierrepont (Baron Pierrepont and Viscount Newark from 1796, 1st Earl Manvers from 1806) 1788-1816.*

Land and Property see Corporate Estates; Private Estates; Town Common

Leisure Amenities

On the whole the Corporation left the famous diversions of Bath to private enterprise. In 1699 it did however assign an area of the Town Common for a public ride and from 1722-3 paid an annual rent to the owner of Claverton Down so that visitors might take outings there. In the later period it felt some responsibility for music at the Pump Room, formerly the Master of Ceremonies' whole prerogative, because the morning performances were thought to attract vital custom to the city centre. These apart, the authorities intervened in the entertainments solely over law-and-order issues, e.g. to stop illegal gambling or crowd-rousing activities like pugilism and cock fighting - though outside the Liberties they had to rely on the Bathforum justices.

Liberties of Bath

Strictly speaking the powers of the Mayor and magistrates of Bath stopped at the borough boundary, a zone defined by the Charter and known as the Liberties. Despite the Corporation's success in 1590 in extending this zone to include Barton Farm, much of the adjacent parish land remained technically outside Bath (and hence came under the county authorities - specifically the Bathforum J.P.s) until as late as 1835. The boundary line, as described in the 1590 Charter, ran along what are now Julian Road and Guinea Lane, swung round St Swithin's to meet the Avon, and then followed the river downstream as far as its confluence with St Winifred's brook where it bent north, passing behind where Marlborough Buildings would later stand, to rejoin Julian Road. (On this western side the boundary bisected the Town Common.) In 1769 a local Act of Parliament added to the Liberties a portion of Bathwick, a fairly small tract that the Corporation nonetheless remembered to include in its future perambulations of the city bounds. Even then the whole borough encompassed no more than the parishes of St James, St Michael, and the Abbey (i.e. St Peter & St Paul), plus Inner Walcot and that one bite into Bathwick near the river. But as urban Bath expanded across its notional boundaries, the administrative status of the rest of Walcot and Bathwick, to say nothing of Lyncombe and Widcombe, became increasingly anomalous. Physically linked and in dozens of ways bound up with the spa's fortunes, they were still legally distinct, which meant for example that the various Bath Improvement Acts did not apply to them, so that both Outer Walcot and Bathwick were forced to obtain Acts of their own. In practice, however, there must have been close cooperation, official and unofficial, between the various local authorities, one example being the permission given to the Bathforum magistrates in 1795 to hold their sessions at the Guildhall.

••• See also **Processioning**.

Licensing

Alcohol could not be sold legally except from premises licensed by the magistrates. Usually in December, adjournments of Bath Quarter Sessions were reserved for the annual 'Brewster Sessions' when city victuallers and publicans came in person before the Mayor and one J.P. to obtain their 'recognizance'. This was a permit granted in return for a forfeitable £10 pledge and a solemn promise to adhere to the true assize (i.e. fair measures and quality) in selling drink and other victuals, to keep an orderly house, to forbid unlawful games, and to remove anyone drunk. These Guildhall Sessions could stretch over several weeks or be largely completed in a day, as in 1776-7 when 132 named premises, including most of the inns and coffee houses, were licensed on 3 December. The right to license, and with it the power to close down unwanted or rowdy alehouses and gin-shops, was an important weapon of municipal control which the authorities were increasingly prepared to wield.

Licensing sedan chairs, bath chairs, and from the 1770s wheeled invalid chairs was another Corporation 'prerogative'. Again it was a yearly procedure, with the chairmen having to turn up at the Guildhall in their usual working pairs. The 1707 Bath Act imposed a charge of up to three shillings for a 12-month licence and a stiff fine of 13s.4d. per offence for carrying an unlicensed chair or, by implication, one not bearing its certified identification number. Chairmen were notoriously quarrelsome, but if fines and suspensions failed to restrain them, the ultimate sanction of loss of licence - and livelihood with it - surely did. The more chairmen there were (c.330 by the 1790s), the more need of careful record-keeping, but one useful by-product was the roster of chairmen's names and numbers posted up in the Pump Room in case of complaints. In much the same way, licensing porters and basketwomen gave market customers some protection by authorising up to fifty named carriers to deliver goods to houses. From 1746 those designated had to wear an official brass badge, and from 1749 any unlicensed carriers were fined. The formal enrolment of apprentices and freemen was also a species of licensing, and from time to time the magistrates dealt with other kinds too - certificates for Nonconformist meeting houses, for example, or the odd prosecution for unlicensed dealing in Excise commodities such as tobacco, spirits and tea.

••• See also **Sedan Chairmen**.

Lock-up and Guard House

The small structure in which drunks, brawlers, and suspect criminals were held overnight before being charged was traditionally known as the constables' cage, and indeed may well have had prominent iron bars. It long stood in the Marketplace next to the public water fountain, but was moved in 1722 to the north side of the Walks (later Orange Grove) and developed into a proper guard-house or police station. It contained a fireplace and must have been manned at least during the hours of the night watch (21.00-07.00 in the winter months, 22.00-04.00 in summer). Sentry boxes stood at strategic points around the town for the watchmen to return to between beats, and Walcot parish established a lock-up of its own in Lansdown Road in 1793.

Loyalist Association

Well-publicised celebrations at the accession of George II in 1727-8 finally helped Bath expunge its old reputation for Jacobitism and prove its Hanoverian allegiance. For the rest of the century no occasion was missed to highlight royal and patriotic occasions with flags and bells, grand illuminations, loyal toasts and entertainments, and humble addresses to His Majesty. By 1734 even the London press could declare Bath 'never so gay, never more loyal' and the theme was endlessly repeated. But if the city stood 'pre-eminently forward in its loyalty to the House of Brunswick' (*Bath Journal* March 1789), its more radical citizens still sought constitutional and electoral change. Two middle-class Bath reform societies and a branch of the more working-class London Corresponding Society were active by early 1793, but their voices were soon drowned out by a new body with a give-away title, the Bath Loyalist Association for Preserving Liberty, Property and the Constitution. Like a host of similar reactionary associations which sprang up at this juncture, the Association fed off current anxieties about the war with revolutionary France. Endorsed, even orchestrated, by the Corporation, it rejected above all 'the wild Doctrine of EQUALITY' and unreservedly supported Mayor Moysey in banning 'levellers and republicans' from meeting at the Assembly Rooms in December 1792. The Association's book was left at the Guildhall for loyalists to sign and soon recorded over 6000 names, a broad cross section of Bath support and including all 326 sedan chairmen (the authorities' reserve weapon, the special constabulary in waiting). This proved to be the moment of maximum public impact. Thereafter, the Association simmered patriotically in the background only to emerge briefly in 1797 to stimulate militia recruitment. It had no obvious connection, though, with the Committee formed in early 1798, when a French invasion seemed imminent, to support a national defence fund to which a very wide spectrum of Bath inhabitants contributed. All along the Loyalist Association probably preached to the converted and it quite failed to crush dissent. Reformists still met secretly, seditious literature circulated, and as late as 1799 the magistrates were trying to suppress disloyal prints on sale at Bath shops.

Lyncombe and Widcombe

The administrative line that split the parish off from Bath ran down the middle of the Avon, so that once a fugitive 'got behind the bear' (one of the stone figures at the south end of the bridge) he was beyond the reach of Bath justice - if still potentially at the mercy of the Somerset magistrates who held sessions at the nearby *Angel* (or sometimes, earlier, at the *Greyhound*). Indeed many of the seasonal beggars that so taxed the Bath authorities slept safe overnight in Holloway, as did the colliers and their scrawny asses who delivered coal round Bath door to door. The parish's whole economy was intimately bound up with Bath's whatever the official divide. Dolemeads wharf supplied the stone from which Georgian Bath was built. There was much cross-holding of properties, and some Corporation members had important interests across the river. E.B. Collibee, for one, held the land needed in 1756 for reservoirs serving the city's Beechen Cliff water supply. Similarly the churchwardens of two city parishes, Abbey and St James's, owned the ground in Widcombe on which their joint poorhouse was built in 1779-81 - a move that almost seems a retaliation for the Holloway beggars. The Lyncombe and Widcombe churchwardens objected, but the fact that their vicar was also Rector and Archdeacon of Bath scarcely helped their cause. This ecclesiastical link never led to a civic one at this stage, though the parish had begun to realise the need for better policing, lighting, paving, and access to justice. Local property owners debated the question at the *Angel* in December 1791, but unlike their counterparts in Walcot and Bathwick they never applied for a special Act of Parliament. At the same time they must have resisted throwing in their lot with Bath, for a resolution of the Council in 1792 to enlarge the city boundaries still excluded the whole of Lyncombe and Widcombe.

••• See also **Liberties of Bath**; **Social Problems**; **Water Supply**.

Magistrates see Justices of the Peace

Market

The right to hold a provisions market twice a week was one of the borough's earliest franchises. Ignoring any literal interpretation of his title 'Clerk of the Market', the Mayor delegated its everyday management to the Bailiffs, who took the profits from letting out standings. They in turn had the assistance of a paid Deputy Clerk from 1767. Despite the increase in food shops at Bath, the market remained vital to the distribution of perishable produce, both wholesale and retail, for an area maybe ten miles round. It is hardly surprising the Corporation took it seriously. Indeed the two were associated physically, for the old Guildhall occupied the upper storey of the market house, and the new one of 1777 still found itself surrounded by the market on three sides. This redevelopment had begun in 1745. The old, open-sided market house was functional enough, equipped with water supply, weighing machine, official measures, and a market bell to signal the start of trading, but it seriously impeded traffic on a main route through Bath, especially on full trading days when stalls, basket traders, horses, carts, and gear of all kinds spilled across the Marketplace. The butchers' market or shambles already occupied a yard off the east side, and in 1745 a £500 donation from Wade, one of Bath's M.P.s, enabled it to be enlarged and fitted with permanent stalls. The green or vegetable market came next, c.1762-3, located further south and equipped with roofed stalls in two rows of five. About the same time a weigh-house was built for hides and skins, and over in Sawclose the Corporation installed a heavy weighing machine for bulky goods such as hay, straw and coal. The Bath Act of 1766 sanctioned the removal of the rest of the market, but further progress depended on protracted arguments over the new Guildhall site.

Farmers, poulterers, fishmongers, market gardeners, and anyone else bringing goods to market had always been exempt from the rules against interlopers, but other statutes and bylaws did apply. Central to the whole concept of the market was fair trading, so that any attempts at profiteering by cornering the market, hoarding, or illegal resale had to be strenuously resisted. Artificial monopolies forced prices up especially in years of scarcity and it was at these times that the Corporation, fearing food riots, most often spoke out against 'forestalling, engrossing and regrating', all practices that distorted free supply and demand. Even in good times abuses crept in, but Council officials did make periodic inspections of produce on sale and checked weights and measures, occasionally burning a sample of rotten meat or confiscating underweight butter and giving it to the poor. Around 1746 the Corporation first licensed market porters and basketwomen (carriers of customers' purchases) and made them wear a brass badge, but it was in the wake of the food shortages of 1765 that it sought better control of the market by re-siting it physically, appointing a Deputy Clerk or Constable of the Market, and issuing a string of fresh orders about trading hours, stall hire, public scales, traffic congestion, and obstructive sacks of grain, piles of cabbages, and carcases of meat. Hours of business were announced by the Town Crier ringing the market bell, with later hours for fruit and vegetables than for animal produce. From 1767 the market became daily (some days with reduced hours), but in 1776 reverted to the traditional Wednesday and Saturday (Friday for fish), open 5 a.m.-11 p.m in summer, two hours shorter in winter. Butter and eggs were available any day bar Sunday - when only mackerel and milk could legally be sold.

Around 1775 the entrepreneurial Councilman T.W. Atwood forced the issue of the new Guildhall by starting building work on the main site. He reconstructed the riverside slaughterhouses, put up a pork butchers' hall, roofed the dairy market, and on Atwood's sudden death Thomas Baldwin completed the lay-out. The result was a crescent of neat, numbered, covered stalls that wrapped round the Guildhall, approached by formal entrances off High Street. Visitors had always lavished praise on the Bath market's rich and varied display, but henceforth it was in superlatives. Two or three hundred traders already rented standings there and their number kept growing. The Corporation felt proud of its showpiece, which in Richard Warner's view was better designed, managed and provisioned than any other market in the country. Of course periodic bad harvests could not be ruled out, when provisions grew scarce and prices rose. Emergency measures were needed in the food crises of 1795 and 1800-1, and in 1800 the Corporation launched a toll-free Saturday grain market in the hope of reducing bread prices. The experiment was not a complete success but foreshadowed the opening of the Corn and Cattle Market in Walcot Street in 1811. Much earlier (from 1736) a Wednesday beast market had been held for a time in Sawclose.

••• See also **Assize of Bread**; **Bailiffs**; **Fairs**; **Guildhall**; **Weights and Measures**.

Master of Ceremonies

Beau Nash was not dubbed 'King of Bath' for nothing, yet he had no official position vis-à-vis the Corporation and owed strict allegiance solely to the polite company at Bath whose spokesman he was. The part he played in civic affairs during his lengthy reign (1705-61) was altogether more complex than this suggests, as he bridged the yawning social gulf between the visiting gentry and the burghers who ran the town. Whether he advised on the improvement of amenities (building the first Pump Room, for instance) can only be guessed at, but by taking charge of the amusements, calming the wilder forms of visitor conduct, promoting sociability, and acting as supreme arbiter of spa protocol, he served a function that the Mayor and his colleagues were ill-equipped to undertake. Profligate and extravagant though he seemed, Nash was also Bath's finest publicist. He undoubtedly brought in business (especially among the wealthy gambling set), and his fund-raising skills for good causes (the General Hospital above all) were legendary. Provided he took care not to trespass on the Corporation's own interests, he enjoyed surprising freedom of action - demonstrated during the Jacobite rising of 1745 when he purchased a set of 21 cannon and fired off defiant loyal salvoes from Simpson's Garden. He ran the music in the municipal Pump Room, often ordered bellringing, sponsored fireworks, erected public obelisks, even, it was said, saved Bath from having to billet troops for a time. Friend of royalty, Nash at his height was unassailable. The Corporation rewarded his massive services to the city with an honorary freedom, and ultimately with a pension and a grand civic funeral.

None of Nash's successors had anything like this clout or charisma. Only with William Wade (1769-77) was the dignity of the M.C.'s office re-emphasised, but his authority too was questioned, especially over arrangements at the new Upper Assembly Rooms. After Wade the role split in two, with separate M.C.s for the Lower and Upper Rooms. It was a necessary division of labour given the longer high season, the increase in visitors, and the heavy programme of entertainments, but it inevitably reduced the office's wider influence. Still, the M.C.s remained important figures. Wearing their badges of honour, they performed their part - petty monarchs of the spa scene; ruling on public etiquette, dress and precedence; setting the tone; mediating, advising, introducing, creating a charmed circle of privilege and show. Their contact with the Corporation, though, was now minimal, and this separateness was emphasised in the sometimes fiercely contested elections by which M.C.s gained appointment - elections in which all the genteel company currently at Bath had voting rights, but from which the town was utterly excluded. Exclusion applied equally to the Assembly Rooms - from which men of trade, including most of the Corporation, were on principle debarred. The growing social aspirations of Bath's commercial and professional élite had to find expression all the same, and the new Guildhall was to provide the setting. Around 1779 the first series of municipal balls took place in a banqueting room as magnificent and flamboyant as anything the Assembly Rooms could offer. And just as telling was the appointment of a suitably qualified Master of Ceremonies to officiate at these fashionable city assemblies. Apart from this highly symbolic function it seems the Guildhall M.C.s had no other duties.

••• For a list of Masters of Ceremonies 1703-1805 see T. Fawcett, *Bath Entertain'd* (Bath, 1998), p.10.

Master Tradesmen

Before 1800 most business enterprises at Bath were small-scale. Even Ralph Allen's stone mines, Stothert's engineering works, or the principal inns employed only moderate mumbers, and a more typical workshop or retailing firm perhaps seldom exceeded a dozen assistants, journeymen and apprentices. Many were smaller still. An individual master (or sometimes mistress - as when a widow carried on her husband's occupation) had limited impact on the market, but in combination they carried much more weight. By organising cartels they could reduce costs, standardise prices, fix wages, exclude non-freemen, prevent the poaching of staff, and fine or sue offenders. Formal structures also gave members the chance of leadership and office, seen most obviously in the nine self-regulating Companies which at their peak (1752-65) covered some of the city's leading trades. The Glazby judgment of 1765 removed their chief justification, though (maintaining the freemen's monopoly), and the system then disintegrated. In future employers would join forces for two main reasons: to hold down wage costs and to keep their prices in line. (Examples of masters' common resistance to demands for wage increases can be found under the entry for **Journeymen**.) General price agreements turn up especially in the service sector. Thus the city lodging-house keepers announced jointly in 1764 they would no longer reduce their rates in midwinter, and in 1783 that they would henceforth charge for the use of linen. The circulating libraries raised their tariffs in concert on three occasions (1773, 1789 and 1797). Coach proprietors sometimes did the same (as in 1783), but the stablemasters were divided in 1793 over whether to increase their common charges for horse and carriage hire. In a free enterprise economy anyone could break rank, but the pressure to conform was strong. When the city publicans, meeting at the *Bear* in December 1792, agreed to deny their premises to radical clubs, they surely assumed that their licences would be at stake for non-compliance.

••• See also **Apprentices**; **Freemen**; **Journeymen**; **Trade Companies**.

Mayor

The mayoral year began in October, several weeks after his election, and was inaugurated with some pomp - a dignified civic procession and a service at the Abbey Church, followed by an elaborate feast for the Corporation and a select list of guests. Pupils from the Grammar and Bluecoats Schools always took part in the parade (the respective

head boys making speeches in Latin and English), and for a few years
the resurgent trade companies joined them. The lavish dinner at mayor-
making and other Mayor's treats were at one time paid for directly by
the Corporation, but following a clamp-down on expenditure in 1731-
3 they were covered by the office-holder himself out of his stipend.
Payments to the Mayor began with an annual sum paid from 1713-14
on the loss of his traditional perquisite of being able to offer the city
freedom, for the usual fee, to a non-apprenticed tradesman. It rose to
£76 10s. in 1733, £100 in 1742, 200 guineas in 1767, and 300 guineas
in 1783 before being cut back, along with banquets, in 1789-93 when
costly city improvements were in full swing. Banquets were
abandoned altogether during the hardships of 1800-1 and Mayor
Atwood gave up his whole allowance (by then 400 guineas) as a result.
Plainly the Mayor's stipend was tied to his hospitality (and by
implication to civic prestige), since he was not otherwise recompensed
for shouldering such a burdensome, seven-days-a-week office.

    To become Mayor one ascended the usual promotional ladder of
Councilman, Constable, Bailiff, Alderman, and often Chamberlain too,
which meant that most incumbents were at least middle-aged on
reaching the top. In 1787 it was the Recorder's view that any Council
member might serve as Mayor, but in practice the office rotated among
the current Aldermen. The result was that in the course of the century
some served two, three, four, or - in the exceptional case of John
Chapman - six times. Families prominent and self-perpetuating on the
Council inevitably produced many Mayors, so that 17 individual
Chapmans, Atwoods, Bushes and Collibees together filled the post 35
times between 1701 and 1800. As time went on Mayors came from
higher social brackets. Where most had once been prosperous common
tradesmen, their successors were as likely to be a physician, surgeon,
laceman, bookseller or banker. The commonest occupation throughout
was that of apothecary (some 15 different Mayors). The rise in

gentility is well illustrated by John Palmer, Mayor in 1796-7. A century earlier the Mayor who had welcomed Princess Anne (and been scolded by Queen Mary for doing so) was sneered at by the Court as a mere tallow-chandler. Yet in January 1797 we find a tallow chandler's son, John Palmer, politely hosting a Guildhall ball for the Prince of Wales and other royals at which the Hereditary Prince of Orange danced all evening with Palmer's own daughter. It hardly needs saying that Palmer was of course by then a gentleman, patentee of the Theatre Royal, a famous mail-coach entrepreneur, and a prospective M.P.

Most of the Mayor's duties were workaday rather than glamorous. He was chief executive, chief justice, returning officer at parliamentary elections, and *ex officio* both Coroner and Clerk of the Market (the latter task effectively delegated to the Bailiffs). He presided not only at inquests and magistrates' hearings, but over the Court of Record, borough Quarter Sessions, and all Council meetings - where he had a casting vote (but not a double vote as one Mayor tried to claim in 1702). He often sat on important Council committees and was ultimately responsible for efficient municipal administration, law and order, and the city's wider reputation. Mayors such as Richard Ford and Ralph Allen stand out as keen administrators - Ford pushed through measures in 1731 to free the city treasury of debt and Allen tried in 1742 to reform Council business. In 1760 Francis Hales injected a new sense of urgency about the dilapidated state of the Guildhall. Others made a name for their courtroom skills, for attempting to deal with social problems (vagrancy; disorderly ale-houses and gin-shops; illegal gambling), or for promoting city improvements. During the politically fraught 1790s Abel Moysey and Henry Harington took a particularly hard loyalist line against radical protest. One ex-Mayor, Leonard Coward, left the Improvement Commissioners the munificent bequest of £10,000 in his will.

As chief executive as well as representative of the Corporation, the Mayor had to deal officially with the Court, Parliament, Government ministers, county officers, or the Mayors of other boroughs, any of whom might communicate with him direct. Similarly addressed to him came a mix of requests, complaints, advice and information from local organisations and individuals, the more pressing of which he brought to the Council's attention. When royal visitors were in town he had to be particularly solicitous. In the event of municipal clashes with powerful figures and interests (e.g. a Queen's household official in

1703, the Earl of Stanhope in 1746, the Pulteney and Kingston estates at various times) or in legal actions (e.g. Chancery and King's Bench suits), the Mayor was personally indemnified, and at all times he had the Beadles to call on for his physical protection. It was not a lonely office, however, and every Mayor must have worked in close cooperation with his chief aides, especially the Town Clerk, Chamberlain, Bailiffs, and his fellow J.P.s - one of whom was always the Mayor preceding. Ideally he took his oaths of office before the Recorder, but otherwise travelled to the Somerset Quarter Sessions to do it. Court requirements might also take him to the County Assizes. In view of the Mayor's multiple functions, any lengthy absences from Bath or any incapacitating illness (two Mayors died in office) must have disrupted business and decision-taking, but only from 1794, authorised by the new Charter, could a Deputy Mayor be appointed.

••• See also **Coroner**; **Corporation**; **Council**; **Court of Quarter Sessions**; **Court of Record**; **Justices of the Peace**.

••• For a list of Mayors 1655-1799 see R.Warner, *The History of Bath* (Bath, 1801), pp.212-4.

Members of Parliament

Bath, which returned two Members, was a fairly open constituency in the sense that it remained one of the very few corporate boroughs whose elections for much of the century were not controlled by wealthy patrons. Nevertheless the Duke of Beaufort (grandee of nearby Badminton) did assist the Tory candidate Codrington win his seat in 1710, the Earl of Camden imposed his own son, J.J. Pratt, on the constituency in 1780, and votes could more or less be bought through favours to local worthies and donations to city improvements. It was money from Gay, Wade and Ligonier that enabled the old Guildhall to be sashed and wainscotted, altarpieces erected in the Abbey Church and St Michael's, and the obstructive north and south gates demolished. Wade also flattered the Corporation by commissioning two sets of civic portraits to hang in the Guildhall where, at city expence, his own full-length likeness was also displayed from 1731. Behind the scenes, as loose political groupings formed behind particular candidates, powerful insiders like Ralph Allen knew how to pull strings. Wade, Henley, and the elder Pitt in 1757, all owed much of their electoral success to Allen, and Allen admitted in 1763 that he was recommending Sebright for the seat 'to my friends in the Corporation'. Quiet manipulation of this kind spoilt the chances of Joseph Langton of Newton Park and Walter Long of South Wraxall on several occasions. All this was possible because voting was restricted to the thirty members of the Corporation, which made the city's representation in Parliament 'as complete a political farce as that of Old Sarum', to quote one commentator in 1792. Attempts to overturn this Guildhall monopoly (most notably in 1705 when the freemen elected their own pair of M.P.s) had always ended in failure, leaving the citizens at large completely disenfranchised until the reforms of 1832.

The Corporation exercised their independence by choosing M.P.s of national reputation or with strong local ties. Wade, Ligonier and the elder Pitt brought special prestige to the city. Scourge of the Jacobites, Wade was immensely popular during the Whig heyday, and during the Seven Years' War too Bath took great patriotic pride in its pair of M.P.s - Pitt, the implacable First Minister, and Ligonier, commander of the armed forces. Even after he quarrelled with Allen in 1763 the 'great Commoner' Pitt still retained much local support, but then in 1766 outraged his Bath constituents, who had lately commissioned his portrait for the Guildhall, by resigning and accepting an earldom. Four other Bath M.P.s - Henley, Ligonier, Thomas Thynne and Pratt - also resigned, but uncontroversially, on elevation to the peerage or higher office. Most of those chosen to represent Bath supported the government of the day (and even held office), though political circumstances took some (Pitt himself, as well as Smith and Moysey) into the opposition at times. By the end of the century the two Bath M.P.s had come to represent more obvious party interests, one Tory (monopolised by the Marquis of Bath's family), and one Whig (controlled from 1801 by the Palmers). Having the minister's ear presumably helped M.P.s put across the Corporation's case when Bath sent 'instructions' up to London - to support specific Bath Bills or measures promoting commerce, or to oppose unwanted legislation (e.g. Pulteney's turnpike proposal in 1771, or the repeal of the Test and Corporation Acts in 1790). The Members were similarly called on to present petitions to Parliament and, on at least fifteen occasions, loyal addresses to the royal family. Such demands were taken seriously. Even illness did not deter Moysey, for example, from attending the Commons in 1788 to vote for a repeal of the Shop Tax, so much detested at Bath. But if M.P.s did the Corporation's bidding, they were less beholden to other citizens. Thus in 1792 the petition urging the abolition of the slave trade, bearing over a thousand local signatures, had to be presented to Parliament by the Somerset M.P.s since Bath's own representatives Pratt and Thynne (respectively Viscounts Bayham and Weymouth) were, like the Corporation, unsympathetic. Two years earlier Pratt and Thynne had rewarded their Corporation electorate with a grand supper and ball, when Thynne had opened the dancing with Mayor Horton's daughter. In this they were following precedent, since lavish Guildhall entertainments had been given by previous M.P.'s - Henley in 1752, Ligonier and Pitt in 1761, Sebright in 1763 and jointly with Smith in 1768, and both Moysey and Pratt in 1780. Some six hundred of the 'chief inhabitants and gentry' attended Moysey's event, and Pratt invited perhaps even more to a ball at Gyde's Rooms and supper in the illuminated and festooned Guildhall, with sedans to ferry his guests between the two.

••• See also **Acts of Parliament**; **Elections**; **Parliament**.

••• **List of Members 1700-1800**. *Alexander Popham 1698-1707; William Blathwayt 1693-1710; Samuel Trotman 1707-20; John Codrington 1710-27 and 1734-41; Robert Gay 1720-22 and 1727-34; General George Wade (later Field-Marshall) 1722-48; Philip Bennet 1741-47; Robert Henley (knighted 1756) 1747-57; General Sir John Ligonier 1748-63 (Field-Marshall and Irish peer 1757); William Pitt 1757-66; Colonel Sir John Sebright (later General) 1763-74 and 1775-80; John Smith 1766-75; Abel Moysey 1774-90; John Jefferys Pratt (aka Lord Viscount Bayham) 1780-94; Rt Hon Thomas Thynne (aka Viscount Weymouth) 1790-96; Sir Richard Pepper Arden 1794-1801; Hon (Lord) John Thynne 1796-1832.*

Militias and Volunteers

Ever since the early 1660s the Lord-Lieutenant of each county had been legally required to raise, arm and train a local militia, in other words a citizen's defence force or home guard to call on in case of rebellion, riot or invasion. But though such local forces were regarded as far less dangerous to civil liberties than maintaining a standing army, and far cheaper too, in peacetime it was hard to fund and motivate them or keep them up to strength. The amateurish Somersetshire militia had performed badly during the Monmouth

Rebellion and by the 1690s Bath had ceased bothering to collect the 'militia money' it was assessed for. We hear nothing of a specifically Bath troop until 1727-8 during the George II festivities, when the jeweller Thomas Goulding briefly captained a rather theatrical body of grenadiers who several times marched through the streets and saluted the visiting Princess Amelia on her birthday with musket fusillades. They soon disbanded, and the Jacobite crisis of 1745-6 found the city without even a token military presence to oppose the Scottish invasion. Hurriedly the Corporation offered £600 towards army recruiting in the south-west, while Beau Nash procured 21 Bristol cannon. Early in 1746 Ralph Allen went further by enlisting a private company of a hundred guards. Under three officers and four NCOs, these held field exercises twice a week and must have made a brave show, in blue uniforms lined with red, as they drilled in Dolemeads or paraded in the Marketplace, drums rolling, before marching back to Prior Park. The troop disbanded regretfully in October 1746 after mustering one last time at the Abbey thanksgiving service and having cost Allen some £2000.

The outbreak of the Seven Years' War revived militias nationwide. In 1757-8 Parliament fixed the Somerset quota at 840 men chosen by lot - though exemption from service was permitted on finding a willing substitute or paying a £10 fine. One of the three officers responsible for training the Bath contingent was the architect John Wood II - no light duty, for the raw force had to be drilled weekly and the military exercises in April 1759, during the French invasion scare, alone took several days. Once the immediate alert was over and peace signed, apathy resumed until the fresh peril of the American War of Independence. As first France and then Spain opened hostilities, home defence again became a priority, and this time unpaid volunteers were mobilised alongside the paid militias. There was talk of forming a Bath squadron of light dragoons, but by September 1779 the city's patriotic youth were joining instead the Royal Bath Volunteers, an armed foot company under the command of Major A. Molesworth. They drilled daily and paraded that December resplendent in white and scarlet and attended by fifes and drums. Not that it was all ceremonial. Within six months they were in action for real, behaving with some gallantry during the Gordon Riots as a mob attempted to set light to the Roman Catholic chapel. The Corporation, originally none too supportive of the Volunteers, now gave them hearty thanks. The battalion saw no war service and stood down in 1783 - as did officers and men of the militias proper who found themselves all at once without a job.

A decade later events began to repeat themselves in the renewed wars with France. Again the militias built up their strength (the Somerset levy being raised to 2960), and again Bath enrolled its share of men into the Bathforum force through parish ballots, their dependents being supported by a Somerset rate on Bath residents. Again the threat of invasion, especially in 1797-8, produced a rush of volunteeers into what was at first called the Bath Armed Association and later the Bath Association Corps of Foot and Horse, since this time it supplemented its four companies of infantry with a more gentrified cavalry wing trained in weaponry by a Bristol swordmaster. Spotting a profitable opening, the Bath firm of Stothert & Co offered to supply equipment and weapons, while local citizens raised funds, rallied support, and sewed marching banners - presented at a parade in Sydney Gardens in 1799. Under Colonel John Glover and seventeen other officers this was the most formidable local guard Bath had yet seen, but as with its predecessor it proved useful above all in backing up the civil authorities at times of disturbances, notably helping to quell food rioting and arson attacks in 1800. Morale wavered at times and desertion was not uncommon. Nevertheless the Corporation valued their contribution and at the short-lived Peace of Amiens in 1802 gave a dinner to the whole force of officers, NCOs and men. In 1810 its gratitude would be confirmed by 50-guinea silver vases presented to Charles Dumbleton and John Wiltshire, the long-serving commanders of the foot and horse.

Night Watch see Policing

Organist of the Abbey Church

As patron of Bath Rectory, the Corporation employed the Abbey organist. In October 1708 the city seal was formally appended to the certificate produced by the organ builder Abraham Jordan on installing a fine new instrument - dominantly positioned on top of the central screen. Jordan himself became the first organist, at an annual salary of £30 (rather than the £15 the Council first thought of) and on the understanding he played every Wednesday and Friday during the summer visiting season and on Sundays and principal saints' days

otherwise. The choice was a temporary expedient, for soon a new organist was in post, a certain Mr Dean, known only from the record of his payment in the Chamberlain's accounts. From then on the succession is clear: Josiah Priest (1714-25, though salaried from 1711), Thomas Chilcot (1726-66), Joseph Tylee (1767-94), and Thomas Field the younger (from 1795) - always at a fixed £37 12s. a year. Considering the organist's commitments (which included helping train the choir of Bluecoats children) the salary was poor enough, but obviously based on the assumption that music teaching, concert performances, and other activities would be his main source of income. Regularly performing on great and small occasions, a skilled executant had ample opportunities to impress potential employers. Not so the humble organ blower, paid a pittance of £2 for a whole year's effort.

••• See also **Abbey Church**.

Overseers of the Poor see **Parish Administration**

Parish Administration

Anglicans, Nonconformists, and Roman Catholics all had their own systems of church organisation, but the established Church of England alone provided a tier of administration, discharged through the parish Vestry, that applied to every resident, Anglican or not. The civil parish formed a unit of local government with both fixed responsibilities (e.g. administering the Poor Law) and potential ones (e.g. lighting the streets). Georgian Bath comprised three full parishes - St James's, St Michael's, and the Abbey (or St Peter & Paul's) - plus the adjacent parts of Walcot parish (Inner Walcot) and, from 1769, a slice of Bathwick. Their Vestries were open organisations to the extent that any male parish ratepayer could attend meetings, speak and vote. In

practice the chief officers and incumbent ministers (of mere curate
status at St James's and St Michael's) wielded strong influence. The
minister, who usually chaired the Vestry, not only appointed his own
Parish Clerk but had a strong say in the Easter election of
Churchwardens who - with the Overseers of the Poor - were the
linchpins of parish administration. But whereas the Churchwardens
owed their allegiance to the Vestry, Overseers and parish constables
came strictly under the city's J.P.s and chief Constables.

Sworn in by the Archdeacon and subject to triennial visitations, the
two Churchwardens looked after the fabric and furnishings of the
church, maintained the churchyard and burial ground, presented the
parish accounts once a year, allocated the rented pews, and (helped by
sidesmen) kept order in church, encouraged and noted religious
attendance, examined cases of bastardy, and reported misdemeanours
of parishioners at large. Their task was particularly onerous during
major rebuilding works, e.g. at St Michael's 1741-2 and 1755, St
James's 1716 and 1768-9, though plans and expenditure always had to
be agreed by the parishioners first - as the minutes of Walcot Vestries,
1770-89, repeatedly show. Above all the Churchwardens served the
views of the parish ratepayer and acted with the two Overseers on
matters to do with the three recognised classes of paupers: the
impotent, the able-bodied, and the work-shy. No parish business was
more sensitive than poor relief, especially in the later eighteenth
century as expenditure rose steeply. The Overseers, upright citizens

approved by the magistrates, regulated both the quarterly collection of poor rates and the weekly distribution of relief (including medicines and the services of an apothecary) to those sick, disabled, infant, aged, or otherwise 'impotent' parishioners who qualified. Other paupers, deemed to be fit or simply idle, were in theory set to work (and if children, apprenticed) or removed to their own parishes - i.e. where they were born or their father had legal settlement. The city Bridewell had once been used to coerce both vagrants and parish poor into productive labour. When that fell into disuse it was left to each parish to establish a poorhouse with a suitable work regime, and again poor rates had to foot the bill. Expenses such as curates' salaries and church repairs were met from pew rents, a parish church rate, and money loans paying interest or annuities. Parishes often ran a deficit. In 1778-9, for example, St James's owed some £3400, which cost more than £200 a year to service, and St Michael's faced heavy costs in its lengthy Chancery suit against the Corporation. Increased Government taxation in the 1790s on top of high poor rates appalled the local Vestries and persuaded them to complain to the Bath M.P.s.

Policing was another burden laid on the parish, carried out at Bath by a petty constable (parish beadle) and up to six tithingmen (deputy constables), nominated by the Vestry but confirmed at the Bath Quarter Sessions and answerable to the Corporation's two (chief) Constables. Their service, onerous enough for men with full-time occupations, apparently lasted for two years with around half the force retiring each year. When on duty they carried staves (formerly halberds), had powers of arrest, and were indemnified by the Corporation. Besides keeping the peace, parish constables had the task of laying information before the magistrates (e.g. on illegal gambling, prostitution, use of unlicensed premises), executing warrants, attending court, assisting the Churchwardens and Overseers (e.g. in collecting rates or dealing with paupers), and making returns of householders qualified for jury service. Parish fire appliances may have come under their remit too. They were paid expenses out of parish rates, and received an extra allowance from the Corporation if called on for special guard or custodial duties. Once the 1738 Act came into force, parishes also supplied a paid night watch, either by rota from among the tithingmen or by additional appointments, to patrol the streets from fixed stands, call the hours, and apprehend 'all Night-walkers, Malefactors, and suspected Persons'.

For a short nine-year period, under the Bath Act of 1757, the separate Vestries were called on to organise their own street lighting, scavenging, and pitching and paving - done through a surveyor of parish highways who contracted out and superintended the provision of these services. This particular experiment in devolved administration gave way in 1766 to a system of Bath Commissioners to which each parish contributed. It was tacit recognition that the existing four parishes were engaged in inefficient duplication of effort and that their role sometimes overlapped anyway with the Corporation's.

A perambulation of the parish bounds, led by the current minister and parish officers (and accompanied by local children to fix the route in their minds), was supposed to be organised at Rogationtide (the week preceding Ascension Day). Such circuits did took place, but except for the Corporation payments towards 'processioning' in Abbey parish, the custom was seldom documented. Other parish activities have left a better trace. By statute baptisms, marriages and burials had all to be registered by the incumbent minister, and the Vestry kept many other records - e.g. minutes of its own meetings, Churchwardens' and Overseers' accounts, parish rate books, lists of paupers, and bastardy orders, some of which have survived.

••• See also **Higher Courts**; **Police**; **Poorhouses**; **Rents, Rates and Taxes**; and under **Bathwick**; **Lyncombe and Widcombe**; **Walcot**.

Parliament

The constitutional settlement of 1688-9 made Parliament sovereign while still enabling the monarch to exert some personal influence over administrations and policies. It was always open for the Bath Corporation to address the King directly, which it often did in congratulatory addresses, but on political, administrative and other matters it went through Parliament and sometimes government ministers. Communication took several forms including petitions to Parliament, instructions to the two Bath M.P.s, drafts of desired local legislation, exchanges of correspondence, and face-to-face meetings between Corporation officers (e.g. Town Clerk or Recorder) and representatives of Parliament and government. Petitioning grew more frequent from the 1760s, with the Council sometimes voting to support or oppose particular local and national Bills - e.g. *for* licensing the

Orchard Street theatre (1767), *for* banning seditious meetings (1795), but *against* the high cost of provisions (1766), restrictions on the Severn fisheries (1778), or routing the Kennet & Avon canal through Bathwick (1796). Ministers could equally well be approached direct, as shown by the Corporation's hint in 1785 to the younger Pitt on the benefits of Palmer's fast mail service. Contact with the two Houses was particularly intense during the drafting and passage of special Bath Improvement Bills when the Bath Members and the Recorder could prove their worth as lobbyists by speaking against the counter-petitions which also flowed into Parliament from the Bills' opponents. In 1788, nervous about their extra-toll-raising Improvement Bill, the Corporation agreed that the two M.P.s - along with Councilman John Palmer and the architect Thomas Baldwin - should first sound out Pitt before proceeding. And a year later, seeing so many objections to different clauses of the Bill from Turnpike Trustees, Wiltshire clothiers, Somerset colliery owners, as well as many Bathonians, they circulated to both Houses of Parliament a printed rebuttal of each point raised. Having refused the arbitration of four M.P.s in this case, the Corporation had to fight its corner by every means at its disposal to get its way. Obtaining such Acts was inevitably expensive, as Outer Walcot discovered over its own Bill of 1793 when Bath Corporation refused to share the costs.

••• See also **Acts of Parliament**; **Members of Parliament**.

Pitching and Paving

Traditionally the main streets been 'pitched' (i.e. cobbled with flat-topped stone setts) with a 'kennel' or water channel running down the middle. Sidewalks, also pitched, were here and there guarded from traffic by lines of posts. Paving proper, with flagstones, probably originated with a new walk (later Terrace Walk) laid out c.1705, though a still better promenade, 27 feet broad, soon fronted a row of shops in Gravel Walks (Orange Grove). Smoother to walk on than setts (and more practical than gravel), pavements gradually extended into other streets frequented by the gentry and in the end they became the norm wherever new streets were laid out. Especially praised was the promenade that by the mid-1740s ran all the way from Abbey Churchyard to South Parade, as easy to stroll on, according to one visitor, 'as in a floored Room'. The improvement of river transport in

1727 allowed Hanham pennant to be carried up to Bath, the result being that by the mid-1730s/1740s this hard-wearing, non-slip sandstone had largely replaced limestone for paving use. Not for pitching though. Limestone or alternatively blue lias, both mined on Bath's doorstep, was much cheaper. Limestone setts probably consolidated the street surface better, though at the expense of breaking up rather quickly under the pounding of horses' hooves and carriage wheels - the reason why heavy, narrow-wheeled vehicles were banned entirely in 1766. Successive Acts of Parliament made first the Corporation (1707-57), then individual parishes (1757-66), and finally the Bath Commissioners (1766 onwards) responsible for pitching and paving, but the actual job of doing it, or paying to have it done, fell on every householder, who had to look after the street opposite the house frontage as far as the middle line. The legislation for Outer Walcot (1793) required that public ways beside and behind a house be pitched and paved as well, while Bathwick (1801) imposed a further duty on residents - watering the pavements between March and September in order to lay the dust. In the case of new developments initial making up of the street would usually be the builders' job.

••• See also **Traffic Control**.

Police

Lists of the 34 'public peace officers' issued in the 1780s include the four Mayor's officers (Beadles), the Town Crier, and the four teams of temporary constables (one petty constable and six tithingmen) from each parish. Essentially it was an amateur, part-time force - as most freedom-loving Britons still preferred, fearful that a regular constabulary might end in a police state. Such light policing depended on other controls to restrain crime - an accepted social order, habits of acquiescience, religious indoctrination, economic dependence, harsh justice - together with the security fostered by close communities and the deterrent presence in so many households of family servants, apprentices, and lodgers. Alhough a thick dossier could be compiled of Georgian criminality at Bath - from pickpocketing, vandalism and malicious assaults up to the worst capital offences and murder itself - it was still accounted a law-abiding place. 'The police is excellent', decided one female visitor in 1794, so that 'ladies may walk in the streets after candle light alone in perfect security'. In daytime the Mayor's officers (and a few private watchmen), at night the parish

watch and a convenient lock-up, coped well enough with ordinary breaches of the peace. Even the threat of arson in 1730 could be handled by the Mayor calling out a posse of 15 petty constables and tithingmen to make a nocturnal sweep of the neighbourhood which picked up 40 vagrants on suspicion. Besides the official police there were always auxiliaries at hand. Ordinary citizens, for example, might play a part - as when Beau Nash launched a hue and cry in 1753 in response to marauding highwaymen on Claverton Down, or the Bath Commissioners in 1790 (and again in 1799) appointed a score of young patrolmen to safeguard the streets until the watch came on duty. Should major trouble loom, the licensed chairmen (over 300 men by 1790) could always be sworn in as special constables, a move which converted a notoriously truculent body of men at a stroke into a 'well-regulated and well-disposed' force - and loyal to boot. Armed with bludgeons, the chairmen were effective in helping restore calm in the aftermath of Bath's Gordon Riots in 1780 but neither they, nor the Bath police, nor even the local Volunteers, could subdue the mob earlier or prevent the burning of the Roman Catholic chapel. Dragoons had to be summoned from Devizes and county militia from Wells, but both arrived far too late, pointing up the spa's vulnerability to mayhem unforeseen. The Volunteers did control a food riot in May 1800 after it had spread from the provisions market, and in October - with the aid of regular troops who happened to be quartered at Bath - managed to disperse a crowd of c.300 hungry Timsbury colliers. Without some such back-up to civil authority the Corporation looked dangerously weak in the face of widespread popular unrest.

••• See also **Beadles; Constables; Crime; Lock-up and Guard House; Militias and Volunteers; Parish Administration; Sedan Chairmen; Society of Guardians; Traffic Control.**

Poorhouses

The idea of reviving the city Bridewell seems to have been given up in the 1730s. As a result, the task of accommodating the destitute and homeless, while at the same time saving on poor relief by forcing all those capable of it to earn their keep, now fell to the parishes. The solution was the poorhouse (or workhouse), a variant on the bridewell idea first permitted by Act of Parliament in 1722. Lyncombe and Widcombe seems to have been the first local Vestry to provide one (1729), near the foot of Lyncombe Hill. Six years later the St James's and the Abbey parishes together purchased a plot just west of Broad Street (actually in St Michael's) for £350 and erected two poorhouse buildings with a surrounding garden and a brewhouse attached. Little is known of the regime here, but inmates were presumably confined (except perhaps for Sunday worship?) and given whatever employment (e.g. spinning) the poorhouse governor could devise. Children above seven would be employed as well, or indentured as apprentices. It is likely that many inmates were people without local settlement rights, for the 'deserving' parish poor increasingly received outdoor relief at home. All paupers were an ever-rising charge on the poor rates, hence the renewed attempt in 1779 to discourage applications for relief by insisting that able-bodied recipients be gainfully employed, and that the rest wear the humiliating letter P (plus parish initial, e.g. PM = poor of St Michael's) on their shoulder, the elderly alone being exempt. By 1800 the cost of each poorhouse inmate (for food, fuel, candles, laundry, etc.) had risen to as much as 5s.8d. a week and steps were taken to reduce what seemed a huge outlay.

The Churchwardens and Overseers of St James's and the Abbey kept their joint Broad Street poorhouse going until 1781. When Milsom Street was built in the 1760s, the developers had been unable to dislodge the poorhouse whose garden ever since interrupted the otherwise uniform terrace. In 1779 the parishes finally agreed to rent out their whole site (for £130 per annum) to Thomas Baldwin who wanted it for Somersetshire Buildings. The two parishes had already acquired land behind Widcombe Parade, despite opposition from the local Vestry, and there they erected a new poorhouse to which the current inmates were eventually transferred. Meanwhile Walcot had established its own poorhouse, built 1768 just east of Weymouth Street. In October 1795 an inquiry found 101 paupers housed there, for whom the 'contractor' or governor was paid about £20 maintenance per week.

By contrast, 294 parishioners were then receiving regular outside relief. Walcot (Inner and Outer) was now far more populous than the other three parishes combined and accounted for more than half the total (over £11,000 c.1800) collected in poor rates. The heavy cost of poor relief (perhaps aggravated by the recent Speenhamland rules for topping up wages) had still done nothing to rid the Bath streets of vagrants. It was this that led Richard Warner, the respected curate at St James's, to invite the cooperation of other parishes in creating a united 'house of industry' (permitted by Gilbert's Act of 1781/2) that would teach the poor the virtues of hard work and at the same time offer economies of scale in running the operation. Though all except Walcot eventually concurred in the incorporation plan, it was never implemented. Indeed not until the 1830s would a union workhouse, embracing many more parishes, be set up in rather changed circumstances. In 1799, after much debate, Walcot had deferred enlarging its own poorhouse because of uncertainty about possible government legislation. St Michael's, however, did act. By 1805, perhaps even before 1800, various buildings in Walcot Street had been turned into a poorhouse. This was distinctly against the wishes of the Corporation which refused any further development, urging the parish to share the Widcombe poorhouse with St James's and the Abbey instead.

••• See also **Bridewell**.

Prisons (City)

In the 1580s the redundant church of St Mary Northgate was put to fresh, rather incompatible uses - the nave and chancel to house the Grammar School, the tower to hold the City Gaol. Both were still there over 150 years later when John Wood complained that the presence of the gaol 'turned the House of God... into a Den of Thieves'. Despite periodic repair and reinforcement (e.g. in 1683 and 1733) the prison tower was never wholly secure. The gaol was 'broken' in 1732; two deserters held there in 1758 sawed through the window bars and killed the gaoler's maidservant in a desperate escape bid; and in 1766 all the prisoners got away by the time-honoured method of forcing the bars and letting themselves down on knotted sheets. Conditions inside were miserable. One inmate complained in 1771 that he had been held almost a year, lacked a bed to lie on, and sometimes went hungry. The wretched quarters he spoke of would be in the so-called 'new' prison, almost certainly the nave of St Mary's. No longer required for the Grammar School, this appears to have been modified for the confinement of debtors in 1768.

By that stage plans for a completely new gaol were under way, thanks to Pulteney's wish to develop Bathwick. Access to his intended new river bridge required demolition of properties on the city side, among them old St Mary's prison. In lieu Pulteney gave the Corporation a plot of ground across the river in Boatstall Mead, and here the Grove Street prison went up in 1772-73. Straddling the centre of the plot, the main block was preceded by a raised terrace reached from the street by a flight of stairs on its south flank. The whole site was damp and flood-prone, as the prison-reformer John Howard recognised during his inspection c.1774, noting also the 'offensive sewers' in the debtors' exercise yard behind the prison block. Howard found that petty offenders occupied four rooms on the rusticated first-floor level and debtors all the upper floors, which included two common rooms (male and female) plus a workshop where debtor prisoners could make items for sale. In 1780 the Corporation leased a further plot behind the prison and walled it round as an extra court. The same year eight Gordon Riot suspects spent several days in the prison pending their removal to Shepton Mallet, and one convicted rioter subsequently passed his last night there before being hanged. As a rule, prisoners charged with felonies, desertion from the army, or other grave offences were incarcerated very briefly before facing the magistrates who would then commit them to Shepton or Ilchester, the county gaols, to await trial. Otherwise the prison typically held a few inmates sentenced for misdemeanours (i.e. minor offences) and a much greater proportion confined for debt or inability to pay the gaoler's fees. After an escape in 1783 (aided by two women visitors) the prison was strengthened, and in 1794 all the perimeter walls were raised and spiked following a further gaol break when five prisoners got away. Only in 1801 was the rear court leased in 1780 finally built on, when John Palmer erected a felons' block of 'solitary cells' running east-west. The number of inmates was increasing and rose again after the Court of Requests increased its powers in 1805. But though the Grove Street prison was already inadequate and costly to maintain, it continued in service for another generation until a brand new gaol at Twerton replaced it in 1842.

It was the debtors the Georgians most pitied, charged for the very rooms they occupied and often short of food and heating. The newspapers resounded at times with their distressed appeals or their thanks to charitable individuals for gifts of bread, beef, coals, and other necessities. Sometimes private benefactors came forward with the sums of money to free them completely, though most charity of this sort was done by the Society for the Discharge and Relief of Prisoners Imprisoned for Small Debts (a Bath branch of the London Thatched House Society), which in January 1777, for example, secured the release of four male and three female debtors (gardener, tailor, journeyman shoemaker, coalheaver, mantua-maker, scourer, and fruiterer) who altogether owed c.£35. Considerable sums were raised in the 1780s-1790s by publicity and appeals (led by the Bath printer William Gye) to relieve debtors imprisoned both in Bath and at the county gaol in Ilchester.

••• See also **Bailiffs**; **Courts of Law**; **Gaoler**; **Lock-up and Guard House**; **Prisons (County)**.

Vignette from The Confin'd Debtor *(1797)*
with Charity directing a cupid to release
a prisoner from the debtors' gaol.

Prisons (County)

Since the city gaol catered mainly for debtors, less serious miscreants, and prisoners awaiting trial by the Bath magistrates, it was left to the county gaols to hold prisoners remanded for the Somerset Sessions and Assizes or convicted for grave criminal offences. Anyone sentenced by the Bathforum (rather than Bath) bench for relatively minor debts and misdemeanours ended up in the same institutions - an increasing category of offenders as more and more Bathonians resided outside the old city Liberties. Unfortunately neither of the main county gaols - the Prison at isolated Ilchester (33 miles away) or the House of Correction at Shepton Mallet - was conveniently reached from Bath which had to bear the costs of transporting prisoners there. Conditions at both places were grim. Ilchester housed both sentenced convicts, inmates awaiting transportation, and dozens of languishing debtors who virtually depended for their survival on Bath philanthropy.   Shepton took convicts on short terms of hard labour as well as many prisoners on remand. Besides periodic gifts of money, food, clothing and fuel, Ilchester debtors received the profits of a special benefit concert at the Guildhall (1787) and the proceeds of William Gye's pamphlet *The Confin'd Debtor* (1797) with its pathetic opening lines: 'From these drear Cells, where horror silent reigns, // Save the dread sound of Groans, and Clank of Chains...'. Inevitably there were occasional escape bids by the convicts, though seldom by the debtors who depended on the gaoler's humanity and lived continually in hopes of salvation through Bath donations. Prisoners remanded by the city J.P.s rarely went to Taunton Gaol, but three suspected criminals who came before a joint Bath-Bathforum bench in 1770 were consigned separately to Ilchester, Shepton and Taunton for the same offence - perhaps to stop them concocting a story together before the trial.

••• See also **Courts of Law**; **Prisons (City)**; **Somerset Assizes and Sessions**.

Private Estates

Next to the Corporation three private landowners held important estates at Bath on the city side of the river - St John's Hospital, the Duke of Kingston, and the lord of Walcot Manor. The Hospital had acquired most of its Bath properties as early as the 13th century or through subsequent exchanges, among them valuable sites inside and outside the walls at the Cross Bath and West Gate which saw important Georgian development and hence increasing rents. Management of the Hospital lands passed from the Corporation to the Master of St John's in 1713, but the two parties continued to do occasional business deals over particular sites, e.g. the acquisitions from St John's in 1751, 1766 and c.1780 to enlarge the main Pump Room, widen George Street, and improve the Cross Bath. Similar accommodations were required with the Kingston estate, which occupied old Priory land southeast of the Abbey Church and likewise surged in value with the fashionable development of Terrace Walk, the Parades and the Abbey Green area. There was some friction with the Corporation over encroachments (e.g. building against the Abbey), the sharing of water supplies (settled by the 1766 Bath Act), and the opening of the Kingston Baths, but the two sides co-operated in 1796-9 during the conveyancing of properties on the east of Stall Street to permit the making of York Street. The manor of Walcot, awkwardly partitioned into Inner and Outer by the city boundary, raised fewer territorial issues because most of the Georgian expansion took place on greenfield sites. After 1750 the Corporation could do little to stem this expansion (except on the Town Common), though they recognised well enough that the creation of the Upper Town threatened the economic viability of central Bath by drawing off custom and undermining land values. Nor could they prevent the Pulteneys developing their Bathwick estate, another potential threat to the centre, and they even colluded in the key move, the building of Pulteney Bridge. By admitting the Pulteneys' right to realise their landed assets, Bath obtained in recompense not only a new prison but very desirable extra water supplies to complement the springs which rose on yet another private estate, the Bruton holdings in Lyncombe and Widcombe. In fact corporate and private interests were not always at odds, and many Council members benefited personally as property owners, tenants, or builders on private lands.

••• See also **Bathwick**; **Corporate Estates**; **Kingston Estate**; **Walcot**; **Water Supply**.

Processioning

By this contemporaries meant the occasional perambulation of the city or parish boundaries to confirm their line, to check for encroachments, and to assert jurisdiction over the area they contained. Little is known about the beating of *parish* bounds at this time, though from 1754 the Corporation periodically gave the Abbey churchwardens five pounds towards the expenses of their processioning days. Corporation inspections of the entire city perimeter - probably activated by the spread of building development north of Cottle's Lane (i.e. Julian Road) - revived in 1776 and thence took place at roughly three-year intervals. Since part of Bathwick now came under the city magistrates, the complete circuit required the Mayor and his company to cross the river twice, but in addition to ordinary boat-hire the use of a barge is sometimes noted in the city accounts. This may have served for the refreshment break: bread, cheese, beer, tobacco, and clay pipes are all mentioned, and on at least two occasions the City Music participated.

••• See also **Liberties of Bath**.

Prostitution see **Social Problems**

Public Health

It was something of a paradox. The very name of Bath conjured up notions of cleansing and healing, yet the place attracted the diseased, crippled, and moribund, which in turn raised the city's mortality rate. As the memorials in the Abbey plainly declared, the waters served very well to lay the dust. Nevertheless it was up to the powers that be to ensure a salubrious environment. Supplying clean water, constructing sewers, paving and cobbling, road sweeping, disposing of rubbish, widening streets, clearing obstructions (such as the city gates in 1754), prosecuting obnoxious slaughterhouses, stopping the sale of rotten meat and fish, these were all measures that helped. The old gibe that Bath lay 'in a bottom', polluted by the sulphurous fumes of its baths, was heard less and less as 'airy' suburbs spread up the hillsides and across the meadows. What sulphur there was came rather from the Somerset coal, whose smoke was already beginning to blacken Georgian buildings. Bath seems to have escaped major epidemics in the period, though smallpox drove visitors away in 1722. The Council had no confidence in inoculation, however, and in 1757 tried to ban its practice within a four-mile radius - which did not stop the procedure being introduced ten years later at Lyncombe Spa. Medical statistics were not kept, so little is known about the wider incidence of urban disease. Slum housing was never inspected or condemned, and low-lying areas near the river suffered from occasional great floods (e.g. 1774 and 1799). A solitary order to the Town Crier c.1723 to kill the Guildhall rats seems to have been a rare instance of vermin control. It seems doubtful whether the solid presence of medical practitioners on the Council did much to improve general public health.

••• See also **Baths and Pump Rooms**; **Infirmaries**; **Scavenging**; **Sewerage**; **Water Supply**.

Pump Rooms see **Baths and Pump Rooms**

Pumper

Once water drinking became a medical fashion at Bath, it opened a new source of revenue to the Corporation who could now profitably rent out the pumps - initially to the two Sergeants-at-Arms but by 1684 to a new official called the Pumper, who took charge not only of dispensing mineral waters on the spot at the King's Bath but also of its extensive outsales. In 1695 he was joined by a second Pumper who supervised drinking at the Hot Bath, but in 1710 the two appointments were merged. It was not a salaried post. Instead the Pumper's income derived from 'acknowledgements' made by satisfied clients and from the trade in bottled waters. Out of this he paid overheads, rates, and an annual rent which rose from £35 in 1695 to £100 by 1705, reflecting the surge in profits that followed Queen Anne's visits in 1702-03. When in 1706 the former open-air pump gave way to an elegant Pump Room, the rent shot up to £200 and four years later to £230 when the Pumper's monopoly extended to the Hot Bath as well. Although this was a sizeable sum to pay, the Pumper's job was reckoned to be a sinecure that guaranteed a good profit. For this reason the post always went to some worthy citizen who was in financial difficulties but had the backing of respectable sponsors. Between 1698 and 1760 the average tenure of eleven successive Pumpers was almost six years each, but from then on the normal term reduced to two or three years. Despite ever-increasing business at the main Pump Room (enlarged in 1751) and the installation of a pump at the Cross Bath in 1748, the rent stayed at £230 until the Corporation, having noticed that extra revenue could be squeezed out of the appointment, successively ratcheted up its annual demands to £300 (1761), £500 (1766), £525 (1777), £630 (1778), £640 (1786), and finally to a colossal £840 (1789), a rack-rent charge which lasted until 1816 when declining profits at the pumps forced a reduction. After 1792 the elected Pumper was always a woman - in Richard Warner's words 'usually the widow of some respectable professional inhabitant of Bath, reduced in circumstances... taking to herself all the profits arising from the pump, which generally allows her to lay by... a competency for her future support'.

The Pumper presided in the Pump Room but other family members and servants assisted. One water drinker around 1751 found himself smitten by the Pumper's entrancing daughter Molly Lawrance: 'She gives us Water, but with each touch alas / The wicked girl electrifies the glass'. Not only good-looking but coolly efficient with it, she was equally praised for her skill in handing out, besides glasses of water, the pills, boluses, drops, draughts, potions and powders variously prescribed to her customers. Pumpers had an onerous task considering all their other duties - from maintaining the premises in good order to acting as a virtual news centre (and keeping the book of new arrivals at Bath). Only the Pump Room music and care of the famous Tompion clock escaped their jurisdiction. Nevertheless, though a reward was expected for services rendered, one Pumper lamented in 1784 that 'many who drank then departed without paying', not perhaps aware of his high rent and short period of tenure. Not surprisingly, some of his successors posted reminders in the newspapers or tried to lay down an actual scale of charges. Long before then different Pumpers had used the London and provincial press to advertise the sale of spa waters. Around 1720 Bath mineral water in quart bottles could be found at a dozen or so outlets in London, transported there by regular wagon services. It then cost an expensive 12s. per dozen but by 1735 the price had dropped to 3s.6d., doubtless under competition from rival English and Continental brands. Fraud was a high risk - even common tap water was sometimes vended under the Bath title - so Pumpers took pains to license particular dealers and to seal every bottle with the city arms and their own name. Eventually they had to compete with artificial carbonated waters as well. Yet with all the hazards and difficulties the office of Pumper continued to be sought after. Not until 1810 was there talk of replacing this semi-charitable position by a salaried administrator, and only in 1823, when receipts were well down, did the Corporation at last discharge the current tenant and attempt to run the baths and pumps themselves.

••• See also **Baths and Pump Rooms**.

Quarter Sessions see Court of Quarter Sessions; Somerset Assizes and Sessions

Recorder

The rather lowly salary of forty shillings a year reflected the fairly nominal services expected of the Recorder rather than diminishing in any way the grandeur of his office, for there was nothing untoward in a sitting M.P. or even a Lord Chancellor serving simultaneously as Recorder of Bath. It was indeed an honour worth repaying on the day of inauguration with a grand supper and ball to the Corporation who had elected him. In return the Recorder was sometimes given prestigious duties. Giles Eyre, for example, made the welcoming speech to the Prince of Wales on the latter's visit in 1738. According to the Charter the Recorder was supposed to be 'learned in the law'. He had the right (in practice never exercised) of voting at Council meetings and, if visiting Bath, the duty of swearing in the new Mayor. In theory he was too a judge in the Bath Courts of Record and Quarter Sessions, even if he seldom sat. Residence was not required, for the holder of the office was actually more useful in London where he could help rally support for parliamentary measures affecting Bath, give a professional opinion, or defend the Corporation's interests if legal and constitutional questions arose. In 1789 for example the first Earl Camden (then President of Council) proved doubly helpful, first in steering the Bath Improvement Bill through the House of Lords and then in advising the Corporation on their case against the Freemen over possible development of the Town Common. Camden, who held the office for 35 years and whose portrait hung in the Guildhall, was close to the Corporation, occasionally attended Council meetings (5 times in 1775), and often gave useful advice. On his death in 1794 his son, John Jefferys Pratt, took over in the same capacity, though for the next few years the latter's role of Lord-Lieutenant in Dublin must have absorbed all his energies. This may well explain the city's keenness to have the power to appoint a Deputy Recorder, finally secured in the new Charter of 1794.

••• **List of Recorders 1700-1800**: *John Trenchard 1696-1723; Giles Eyre 1723-1740; Sir Robert Henley 1740-1758 (M.P. for Bath 1747-57); Thomas Potter (M.P. for Okehampton) 1758-59; Sir Charles*

Pratt, 1st Baron and then 1st Earl Camden (Lord Chief Justice, then Lord Chancellor, then President of Council) 1759-94; Sir John Jeffreys Pratt, 2nd Earl Camden 1794- (M.P. for Bath 1780-94).

Rector of Bath

In becoming Rector he became at the same time Vicar of Widcombe and Lyncombe. He was appointed by the Corporation, who held the benefice and provided the Rector's house by Upper Borough Walls that went with the living. Ever since the consolidation of the existing city churches into a single rectory in 1583, the Rector had been the dominant local churchman, for the ministers at St Michael's and St James's were merely curates whom the Rector himself appointed. Only with the massive development and increasing wealth of Walcot parish from the 1730s onwards did the Rector of Walcot begin to gain comparable influence, and even then his modest base at St Swithin's could hardly match the grandeur of the Abbey Church where the Rector of Bath presided. The latter might have an additional diocesan power base. At least three Bath Rectors - William Hunt, John Chapman and James Phillott - held (at least for a time) the simultaneous office of Archdeacon within the see of Bath and Wells, which in theory required them to make three-yearly visitations to every parish in their district. Another Rector, Thomas Coney, was a canon of Wells. Furthermore both Chapman and Phillott had close family links with the Corporation. It was usually the Rector who preached on special national occasions and at the annual Mayor-making ceremonies when the Corporation processed to the Abbey Church ('gift sermons' that the city paid for), but his curate (or reader) and other local and visiting clergy took many of the regular services, whether at the Abbey or Widcombe. In 1755, when Duel Taylor was Rector, the income was said to be too poor for him to pay his curates more than a pittance, but most Bath Rectors were pluralists with income from other livings besides - Hunt at Chewton Mendip, Coney at Chedzoy and Over Stowey, Chapman at Newton St Lo, and Phillott at Stanton Prior. Phillott made a special effort to improve the living, persuading the Corporation in 1787 to borrow £800 to rebuild the rectory and in 1799 trying to regain property he believed the city had usurped. A proposal in 1773 to upgrade St James's and St Michael's into full rectories was not adopted.

••• See also **Abbey Church**.

••• **List of Rectors 1700-1800**: *William Clements 1681-1712; William Hunt 1712-33; Thomas Coney 1733-52; Duel Taylor 1752-67; John Taylor 1767-68; John Chapman 1768-86; James Phillott 1786-1815.*

Regalia and Symbols

Chief symbol of Corporation authority were the two silver maces, adorned with the royal arms and borne in ceremony before the Mayor by the Sergeants-at-Arms. The old maces, several times repaired, were finally scrapped in 1708-09 when the Chamber allotted £60 towards a new pair, silver-gilt, and allowed the old ones in part exchange. The new maces would be refurbished and twice regilded over the years. In 1738 the Prince of Wales on a visit to Bath presented the Corporation with a salver and a silver-gilt cup which at future Corporation entertainments was solemnly passed round before the toasts. During the same visit the Pumper handed the Prince his glass of spa water in a newly purchased gilt bowl, but this was not added to the city plate. By 1772 the Guildhall still possessed no more than 300 ounces of plate, including a pair of candlesticks, on which to pay duty. The aldermen's red robes, the constables' painted brass-knobbed staves, and above all the maces, denoted the power and dignity of office, but nothing symbolised the legal personality of the incorporated borough better than the simple common seal, which set a binding imprimatur on all important documents. The seal portrayed the city arms or shield in its traditional form, viz. a sword placed on a background of water (above) and wall (below), rather than the heraldic version of 1623 which had wall and water reversed. This potent borough symbol may well have appeared on banners and the like, but the flag flown from the Abbey Church tower (and which the Corporation renewed at intervals) must surely have been the Union Jack. The Mayor had use of a smaller seal, re-engraved in 1777, that went with his office.

Rents, Rates, and Taxes

In and about Bath the custom of leasehold tenure of land still predominated. Revenue from the Corporation's own estate, which in central Bath at least was fairly densely built on, continued to be let for long terms 'on three lives'. This method achieved only a modest return from rents but produced unpredictable windfalls from 'fines' whenever one of the named lives changed on the lease. Other landlords had once let on similar terms, but since their estates were in comparison little developed, the trend here was for lifeholds to give way to short tenancies (sometimes on rack-rents for the maximum profit) and ultimately to 99-year building leases. That was indeed how much of new Georgian Bath evolved - through the steady extinction of long leases, the consolidation of plots, the release of land to developers, the subleasing to builders, and the eventual letting of premises to tenants - the whole mechanism safeguarded by legal contracts and carefully maintained rent rolls. Private landlords such as Kingston and Pulteney employed agents to collect rents quarterly or half-yearly. For the Corporation it seems to have been more of a concerted effort led by the offices of the Chamberlain and Town Clerk, as was the collection of water rent from all householders on city mains supply. From 1774 payment of quit rents was expected twice a year, Michaelmas and Lady Day, at the Guildhall. Although the master rent book was a vital document, no adequate copy of the current volume (Michaelmas 1776 onwards) seem to have existed in 1779-80 during its temporary deposit in London in connection with the St Michael's lawsuit. As a result municipal quit rents went uncollected for that period and had to be pursued later.

In the case of rates the collectors went round door by door, entering payments in small quarterly or half-yearly record books as they walked their rounds. At intervals they remitted their takings to the Guildhall or the Vestry chest. Three sorts of rates were charged - a street rate for services such as 'lamps and scavengers', a church rate to cover church repairs and other expenses, and a poor rate to pay for pauper relief. A statutory city rate for public street lighting and refuse collection had been imposed by the Act of 1707. The latter required magistrates to appoint street surveyors, scavengers and rate collectors, and to agree with the surveyors a quarterly rate. The Act of 1738, besides capping the rate at 8d. in the £, increased the penalty for non-payment from £5 to £10 and levied an extra sum to pay for a night watch - this time assessed by the churchwardens. The next Act (1757) made parishes responsible for lighting and scavenging as well as the night watch, but the major legislation of 1766 reversed this policy. In future the new Bath Commisssioners would provide all these services out of a consolidated rate of up to 1s. in the £, leaving the parish to collect just the church rate (entirely a Vestry matter) and the poor rate (subject to the magistrates' approval). Complaints about poor rate assessments could in theory be heard at Quarter Sessions, but the ever-rising cost of poor relief generally was a nationwide phenomenon with no easy solution.

Government taxation likewise increased in the period and climbed remorselessly in the last quarter of the century to help finance the American and French wars. It took various forms - direct taxes, customs duties, excise and stamp duties, and fees for trading licences. Direct (sometimes called the King's) taxes - the least efficient to collect - consisted of Land Tax (generally at 4s. in the £) and a motley group known from 1785 as 'assessed taxes' that targeted houses, windows, shops, servants, horses, and carriages. Like the poor rate these were all collected at parish level. Moneys received at Bath passed twice a year to the Somerset Assistant Commissioner and so to the Receiver-General in London, but the Corporation may have served an intermediate 'divisional' role since, at least in 1787, the Chamber received a small poundage (percentage reward) on all the King's taxes. In addition they selected the unpaid assessors (the majority drawn from the Council's own ranks) and swore in the collectors, two per parish, who were also remunerated by poundage. If the Land Tax (which could be set against rent) escaped censure, assessed taxes did not. The short-lived Shop Tax (1787), which unfairly penalised Bath, was much resented by local retailers who campaigned hard for its repeal. Similarly, in 1797, word of a projected further rise in the tax on houses and windows - already inflated by an earlier 'commutation' tax - was enough to produce a flurry of Vestry meetings and a direct appeal to government.

But indirect taxation was no more popular, certainly not in a competitive retailing environment like Bath, where Customs officers in one swoop in 1768 on milliners' and drapers' shops netted undutied

Deposition to the Bath J.P.s by James Cross, Excise Officer,
claiming that James Broom of Walcot is concealing
on his premises a quantity of dutiable starch.

goods worth as much as £600. Local traders were indeed sometimes openly warned in the Bath press when government snoopers appeared on the scene. Excise duties - which bore on alcohol, tobacco, salt, candles, soap, starch, glass, leather, and other common consumables - were collected on regular rounds by Inland Revenue employees working from an Excise Office at the *Globe* in Kingsmead Square, who sometimes brought prosecutions before the Bath magistrates. Around 1750 the nearest branch of the Stamp Office appears to have been at Bristol, which was where the Town Clerk obtained his stamped stationery. As the range of stamp duties increased, it paid to employ an agent (of the Somerset office) at Bath, namely H.E. Howse, a High Street draper and later Chamberlain to the Corporation. If Wordsworth in the remote Lake District could make £400 a year as distributor of stamps, Howse surely commanded a still more profitable operation at Bath, given the demand there for legal documents, newspapers, advertisements, playing cards, hats, gloves, patent medicines, perfumes, and gold and silver plate - all requiring stamps. On behalf of the Inland Revenue he also supplied annual dealers' licences and various certificates. Every additional tax or deadline for renewal must have brought brisk business - as in May-June 1795 when 2980 hair powder certificates were issued at Bath alone, doubtless encouraged by the posting of lists of certificate-holders on church doors. Income Tax, instigated in 1799, claimed still more local victims, with householders and lodgers alike expected to declare their income at the authorised office in Fountains Buildings. All in all Bath was no mean contributor to the national Exchequer - in 1799 to the tune of £82,000 in Income Tax alone.

••• See also **Corporate Estates**; **Income and Expenditure**; **Parish Administration**.

Royalty

By 1727 Georgian Bath was effusively royalist, even naming its principal new buildings in royal style (Queen Square, King's Circus, Royal Crescent, etc.) and celebrating accessions, coronations and royal birthdays with gusto. Not a fibre of Jacobitism remained in the Corporate body, the message ran; Bath was Hanoverian through and through, the citizens solid for King and Constitution.

Stuart patronage had given Bath kudos and a measure of political protection, yet as late as 1683-88 the monarch's power to meddle in municipal affairs had been shockingly demonstrated by the forced ejection of Council members and, worse still, the replacement of the precious Elizabethan Charter by one which effectively allowed the Crown to control the Council and which foisted on Bath an alien post of High Steward. There was little choice for the Corporation but to acclaim James II in 1685 and connive in his Catholic policies, but then to switch loyalties once more in 1688 when the Protestant William came to the throne. Safety from royal interference in future came with the freedoms enshrined in the 1689 Bill of Rights - though this would not stop Queen Mary censuring the Corporation in 1692 for their presumption in welcoming her estranged sister, Princess Anne. Once crowned herself, Queen Anne repaid the spa by two full court visits in

1702 and 1703, marking a resumption of traditional Stuart royal favour and boosting Bath's fashionability. But the Old Pretender's rising in 1715, crushed though it soon was, proved that Jacobite sympathies died hard in some Bath quarters. Yet this hardly explains why no reigning Hanoverian monarch ever visited Bath in spite of all the loyal addresses the Guildhall inscribed. The first two Georges shunned the provinces anyway, but George III almost ostentatiously steered clear of Bath while bestowing his favours on nearby Weymouth and Cheltenham.

The spa became associated instead with the (sometimes rebellious) royal offspring. Princess Amelia made the first of her many visits in 1728, her brother-in-law the Prince of Orange in 1734, Frederick Prince of Wales in 1738, and Princess Caroline in 1746. The Corporation honoured these occasions by ceremoniously welcoming their guests at the North Gate, waiting on them with respectful speeches and, in the case of the Prince of Wales, offering a Guildhall banquet and freedom of the city - at the risk of alienating George II for excess of zeal towards an insubordinate son. Several later royals received the freedom too (presented in the traditional gold box), notably the Prince of Wales (the future George IV) and his brother the Duke of York in 1796. They spent weeks in Bath at this time, took the waters, bestowed the royal appointment on fortunate tradesmen, graced the assemblies, wined and dined the Corporations of Bath and Bristol at the Guildhall, and were treated to a sumptuous entertainment by the Mayor in return. Royalty was after all the biggest catch of all at a resort that prided itself on attracting 'the quality' yet found itself increasingly in competition with other watering places. Such prestigious and glamorous visitors brought no political benefits however, and in the later eighteenth century they may have wrongly hinted that Bath was a hotbed of Whig opposition.

St Catherine's and St John's Hospitals see under Almshouses

Scavenging

Keeping the streets clean and disposing of refuse had been Council preoccupations as early as 1615 when a scavenger was first appointed to deal with waste. From 1707 householders were obliged by statute to pay a scavenging rate, sweep outside their property, and store their rubbish until the scavenger (or 'raker') came round with his cart and bell. What he collected no longer ended up on unsavoury middens just outside the walls but seems to have been spread on the Common, but until refuse became a profitable commodity (as it had by 1800) scavenging was seldom efficient and Georgian Bath could hardly be called spick-and-span. Better paving and sewerage helped of course, but the streets were muddy when wet, dusty when dry, and often littered with ashes, organic waste, animal droppings, broken glass and crockery, rubble and dirt from building works, and other general mess. At times bones and offal from the slaughterhouses polluted the river, rotting fruit and vegetables lay about the Guildhall after markets, and piles of rubbish accumulated even on the vacant ground below the fashionable Parades where they were were picked over by Bath's poor for usable cinders and items worth recycling. The walks and smarter streets were nevertheless kept tolerably clean, and once the Bath Commisssioners took control in 1766 they introduced new measures, tried to have the streets swept daily before ten o'clock, provided boxes for dust and litter, issued writs against offenders, and fined the cleansing contractors for any shortcomings. By the 1770s some slackness had already crept in. If towns were to be judged on their neat appearance and care for hygiene, wrote one critic, a great health resort like Bath ought to be quite ashamed of the 'excrementitious filth' that fouled Avon Street and other places. Even politer neighbourhoods suffered from uncollected refuse, servants beating dusty carpets, and urchins scattering ashes. The trouble was that as the threshold of public decency rose, nuisances and eyesores that were formerly overlooked became matters of complaint. It deserves noting therefore that by the 1790s the 'great attention' that Bath paid to street cleansing was at last coming in for praise, even if Mrs Allen (in *Northanger Abbey*) did shun the city's pavements in dirty weather and quite fashion-conscious women clink along the streets in pattens to keep their shoes out of the mire.

Schools

Education at Bath was mainly in private hands - from the dame schools for younger children to the classes run by mathematics and writing masters, the commercial and prep schools for boys, genteel finishing schools for young ladies, and the individual teaching provided by governesses and private tutors. However some schools had a more public character and need mention here.

The Grammar School (i.e. the Free School or King Edward's) had been granted to the city in 1552 in a deal that required the Corporation to maintain both a school and an almshouse (St Catherine's) out of the income from a hundred or so Bath properties. This endowment would have been generous had the Corporation not applied most of the revenue to other purposes, cheaply installing the school in the redundant church of St Mary-by-Northgate (and the city gaol in the church tower) instead of building a proper schoolhouse. There it still was in 1734, a hundred and fifty years later, when its current Master, Walter Robbins, learned about the city's apparent long-standing misappropriation of funds and petitioned the Crown for an inquiry. The Charity Commissioners investigated, upheld Robbins' charge of embezzlement, and rebuked the Corporation for neglect of its trust, but the city fathers ignored the hefty fine imposed on them and only in 1742 agreed to erect a proper building. This New School, occupying the old *Black Swan* site in Broad Street and costing over £4500, was finally inaugurated with civic ceremony in 1754 under the recently appointed Master, Arthur Hele. The Corporation dared not, however, oust the stubborn Robbins who hung on to his old salaried post at St Mary's until his death in 1762, upon which the New School finally assumed the title of Grammar School. At the same time Hele succeeded to the Charlcombe rectory which went with the headship. The Master's meagre salary of around £35 was supplemented not only by this Charlcombe living but by fees from day pupils and boarders. Elected by the Corporation, and necessarily both an ordained Anglican and a first-rate classicist, the Master personally appointed and paid an usher and other assistants to teach the younger boys. Arthur Hele's assistant, the formidable Nathanael Morgan - Master in all but name from 1772 - took over fully in 1778 and burnished still further the Grammar School's scholarly reputation. He followed Eton's classical curriculum, but the school otherwise remained a burgher institution, principally for the sons of solid citizens and freemen. As such it must have spawned an old boy network that ramified through the whole civic body. It was no accident therefore that the Grammar School always figured in the annual procession to inaugurate the new Mayor, permitted a star pupil to crown the occasion with a Latin speech, and in 1785 flattered the Corporation by proclaiming on its banner, next to the city coat-of-arms, that modern Bath was a veritable Athens reborn.

Bluecoats charity-school children took part in the mayor-making as well, and a Bluecoats boy gave a short address in English, but the corporate ties here were weaker. The job of the Bluecoats school was to drill selected boys and girls from poorer families in sound Christian principles and the 3Rs to prepare them at fourteen for apprenticeships and domestic service. Founded in 1711 under the wing of the SPCK but otherwise unendowed, the school depended on philanthropy. Donations must have been ample, for the Trustees were soon lending money to the Corporation at interest and in 1721 raised another £700 from subscribers towards the cost of a proper schoolhouse. Though charity schools remained politically suspect in some quarters, they were seen at Bath as good Whig institutions, so the Corporation readily granted the site on Upper Borough Walls for William Killigrew's new building. Any early doubts had long since been assuaged by the sterling qualities of the founding schoolmaster and mistress, Henry Dixon and Mrs Bell, and by the sight of disciplined lines of uniformed youngsters parading on Sundays at the Abbey Church where in due course they made up the choir. The Corporation had no direct say in running the Bluecoats school, but encouraged it anyway, as did the clergy who every year preached fund-raising sermons. The income also went towards supplying the 80-100 pupils with a school uniform and paid their apprentice or employment premiums when they left. In return the children sang not only in the Abbey Church but at important events such as grand funerals (Beau Nash's for one) and the inauguration of public buildings.

The Sunday schools, by contrast, were a mushroom growth. By October 1785, just nine months after the launch, over 600 children were attending Sunday classes in rooms scattered through the Bath, Walcot, Bathwick, and Lyncombe and Widcombe parishes. Each class took around twenty 6-to-10-year-olds and concentrated as much on instilling docile, respectful behaviour as on repeating prayers, singing psalms, and teaching basic literacy. Instructors were paid, but the system depended too on regular and quite onerous inspections by honorary 'visitors' from the overseeing Committee who could, if necessary, pressurise poor parents into forcing their children to attend. After a double session (9 or 10 a.m. to 1 p.m., 3 to 5.30 p.m.) the classes were marched in line to evening service and a sermon at the Abbey Church where they sat subdued on numbered benches, girls facing boys. Onlookers were sometimes affected to tears by the sight of city urchins so transformed. 'Regular attendance, decent behaviour, a desire to learn, and cleanliness' brought many of the children small financial rewards and also qualified them for the associated School of Industry or even the Bluecoats. First promoted by the 'Stanley ladies' (Maria and Isabella), the weekday School of Industry in St James's Street could soon accommodate 180 older children who, in addition to practising their reading, learned to spin and sew, knit stockings, make nets, and cut out garments - including their own olive-green uniforms - from cloth woven on the spot. But the momentum could not be sustained. Even before 1790 the Sunday schools had peaked (at nearly 800 registered pupils, not counting the children of Nonconformists who had their own Sunday classes). By the later 1790s, despite income from the sale of manufactured goods, charity concerts at the Abbey Church, and private donations, the Church of England schools were falling into such debt that cutbacks, especially in the expensive School of Industry, seemed inevitable. Though the Sunday schools at least did rally, the large monitorial schools established at Bath from 1810 robbed them of their old sense of urgency.

••• **List of Grammar School Headmasters 1700-1800**: *William Baker 1681-1706; William Street 1707-13; Benjamin Wilding 1713-20; Bartholomew Richards 1720-21; Walter Robbins 1721-62; Arthur Hele [Master of the New School 1754-62] 1762-78; Nathanael Morgan 1778-1811.*

Sedan Chairmen

Unlike private sedan chairs and, from the 1770s onwards, an increasing number of invalid wheel chairs, the majority of chairs to be seen on the streets were for public hire. As we know from Stuart visitors, portable chairs had been introduced at the spa long before official licensing came in with the Bath Act of 1707. Already they took two distinct forms: the windowed 'glass chairs', or sedans proper, used for genteel carriage about town; and the smaller, light-framed, short-poled bath chairs, covered in baize cloth, which conveyed patients needing treatment to and from the various hot baths, collecting them from their very bedside if required. By 1700 a score or more of each

type may have been in service and the Act of 1707 permitted the magistrates to license up to sixty, each one painted black with the number in white. The same Act stipulated an annual licence fee of three shillings, penalties for misdemeanours, and a tariff of charges for carrying certain distances or for waiting. Additional legislation in 1720 and 1739 required the chairmen to wait for fares at appointed hire stands and altered the charging system to one by distance - 6d. up to 500 yards, 1s. from 500 yards to one mile. The chairmen seem to have owned their chairs personally and some pairs stayed together for many years. They may have alternated between bath chair and sedan, switching perhaps mid-morning after the early portage of people to the baths. In the 1740s a rather more substantial, waterproof, but still windowless form of bath chair replaced the earlier flimsy type. Though usually hired on the spot, chairs could be booked in advance or rented by the week, and would sometimes transport fragile objects. At night they had to be lit by a lantern or accompanied by a link boy carrying a flaming torch.

The permitted number of sedans grew from 80 in 1755 to a maximum of 250 in 1793-4 when there were 22 licensed stands and 326 individual chairmen. But in spite of detailed regulation and lists of measured routes and charges in Bath guidebooks, disputes still arose. The chairmen had a mixed reputation. A number suffered fines, suspension, and even dismissal for brawling, swearing, drunkenness, refusal to carry a fare, insulting passengers, unserviceable vehicles, and bad attitude generally. Waiting for fares could be tedious (many chairmen had dogs for company) and their work tended to be seasonal. Their sense of solidarity, on the other hand, is evident in the 1790s when they clubbed together to resist a spate of vandalism against their vehicles, and also forced the Corporation to accept fares of sixpence per 300 yards uphill as compared with 500 yards on level ground. As a body they also succeeded in long delaying the introduction of hackney cabs at Bath. The city after all needed their goodwill, for at any whiff of riot the chairmen could be sworn in *en masse* as special constables to reinforce the limited police then available.

••• See also **Licensing**.

Sergeants-at-Arms

The alternative title of Sergeants-at-Mace recalls their function of bearing those symbols of sovereign authority, the city maces, before the Mayor on ceremonial occasions - an honourable, not a menial, office. Yet most of their time was spent quite differently, managing the hot baths and, in a rather bizarre mix of duties, serving the Court of Record. In practice their appointment was permanent, if in theory subject to annual re-election, so that just seventeen Sergeants, two in post at a time, spanned the whole century.

Celia Fiennes noted in the 1680s that they attended the baths to preserve order and decency. In 1675, once drinking spa water became a serious part of the cure, the Sergeants were allowed for a time to profit from the new craze, but by 1684 a new post of Pumper had been created to deal with water drinking and the considerable trade in bottled water. This still left the Sergeants in charge of the hot baths and the large staff of male and female guides, and of 'wet' and 'dry' pumping - medical treatments in which the guides pumped hot water over just parts of the body. As administrators of vital spa institutions the Sergeants enjoyed growing status. According to John Wood I they 'bear the Rank of Gentlemen... preside over the Baths... see that Patients are properly attended, and... prevent... Disorder; for which People of Fortune make them such Gratuity as they think proper.' Clients usually rewarded the Sergeants at the end of their treatment, but since the value of tips varied, the Corporation reminded the Sergeants in 1741 to 'share and share alike' and to alternate between the King's and Cross Baths. The re-launch of the now separately run Hot Bath in 1777 reduced the Sergeants' *ad hoc* earnings, so that after 1783 all fees and gratuities went to the Chamberlain and the Sergeants became salaried employees at a guinea a week each. In 1792, with the Sergeants now responsible for the private baths as well, their annual salaries rose to £100. Even so, in 1801 one of the Sergeants, Samuel Jones, was indebted to the Corporation for £55.

The Sergeants undertook a variety of other duties - witnessing depositions for the Town Clerk, billeting troops, assessing damage claims after the 1780 Gordon Riots, and travelling (once as far as Abergavenny) on Corporation errands - but their main allegiance next to the hot baths was to the Court of Record, this time wearing the hat of Bailiffs' officers and court attornies. Having no legal training they could not plead as full counsel, but seem to have represented the interests of plaintiffs and defendants in the sense of general advisors and guarantors of fair trial. For this were entitled to certain court fees.

••• See also **Baths and Pump Rooms**; **Court of Record**.

••• **List of Sergeants-at-Arms 1700-1800**: *Francis Clist 1690-1702; John Sherston senior 1691-1710 and 1711-19; George Pitman 1702-23; John Sherston junior 1710-11 and 1719-41; Walter Masters 1723-41; Richard Biggs 1741-51; Richard Jacob 1741-51; Thomas Rosewell 1751-56; Richard Prynn 1751-65; James Blatcheley 1756-72; William Smith 1765-75; Richard Jones 1772-75 and 1776-79; Benjamin Axford Jan-Sep 1776; Daniel Lewis 1776-78; William Bridgen 1778-79; Samuel Jones 1779-1803; John McKenzie 1779-1803.*

Sewerage

Ever since Roman times three main drains had transported surplus water from the built-up area and the hot springs to the river. By 1700 the so-called Bum Ditch behind Horse Street (later Southgate) still survived, as the outflow from the Cross and Hot Baths also may have, but the marshy nature of the Ham before the Parades were built suggests that the ancient great sewer running east had become blocked by then. Open channels (or 'kennels') ran down the middle of the main streets, removing surface and storm water and some refuse with it, but few buildings were yet connected to a sewer. Houses had cess-pits which required periodic clearing out by nightsoil men - hence the stinks that visitors complained of.

Laying new sewers began with a private initiative in 1718 when two Corporation members, Thomas Atwood and Walter Chapman, drove a sewer through Upper Walks, i.e the north side of what became Orange Grove. This was not simply an overflow drain since the Council demanded that the nearby public privy should also discharge into it. Aware that sewers, like mains water, could produce income, the

Corporation took to financing them within the old town, starting with a common sewer constructed in 1726/7 the length of Stall Street and down to the river. Sewers rendered the former 'kennels' unnecessary and permitted streets to be cambered and provided with side gutters. It seems, though, that the city undertook new sewers mainly at the request of local householders who would have to pay an annual rent of 10s. or £1 for a 'gout' into the main sewer. Hence the system developed quite slowly, with Westgate Street and Cross Bath Lane not served until 1760-1, and the General Hospital and upper Broad Street from 1764. Most new Georgian developments laid 3′x2′ (later 3′x5′) sewers as a matter of course, some of which interconnected with the older drainage - as in the case of the Parades sewer which received the ancient 'Great Bath Gout' from the King's Bath. Some districts may have lacked proper sewerage until well after 1800 when more Bath residents began installing water-closets. Even in the better-off neighbourhoods blocked drains occasionally caused flooded basements after heavy rain. Contamination of water supplies was also a risk. For example the younger John Wood was in trouble in 1776 for letting his 'foul drain' just west of Royal Crescent flow into the St Winifred's stream that supplied the Town Common farm.

••• See also **Water Supply**.

Sheriffs see **Bailiffs**

Social Problems

Poverty lay at the root of much antisocial behaviour. Bath had a sizeable working-class population, some native-born, many others attracted to the spa by good employment prospects, but demand for labour fluctuated, and illness, accidents, seasonal stoppages, periodic high food prices, and many other causes could easily propel a family into pauperdom. To this there were two official solutions. 'Settled' or native paupers were entitled to parish poor relief (or the poorhouse!), and 'strangers' could be removed to their parish of settlement. Some survived through private acts of charity, the odd public collection, or with help from the Strangers' Friend Society (started 1790), but casual philanthropy was never enough and desperate people turned to other remedies - from street-begging and prostitution to petty crime, alcohol abuse and suicide. Begging and soliciting reached their height in the

main visitors' season, when vagrants, 'trav'lling whores', and opportunists of all kinds flocked in to try their luck.

Vagrancy was an enduring problem at Bath, not least because the entire nation, rich and poor alike, had a theoretical right to the benefit of the healing waters. But if the poor could not be denied, they could at least be categorised into the deserving few and the rest. For this purpose Bellott's and, even more, the General Hospital proved ideal filters by requiring patients to be properly authorised for treatment before setting out from their parishes. This control provided a highly convenient excuse for brusque dealing with any who turned up unauthorised. Speaking of the General Hospital in 1743, John Wood hit the note exactly. Its chief purpose, he argued, was 'to discriminate *Real Objects of Charity* from *Vagrants* and other *Imposters*, who crowd both the Church and Town, *to the Annoyance of the Gentry resorting here*; and who ought, by the Care of the Magistracy, to be Expell'd and Punish'd'. The customary punishment was a whipping by the Town Crier, which even the Mayor, Richard Masters, admitted in 1702 was 'very inhumane to poor creatures'. Vagrants galore were lashed out of town all the same - a punishment sometimes administered on a cart so that bystanders could see better. Yet neither this, nor removing them to their parish, nor ordering them to the Bridewell at Shepton Mallet (which the 1744 Vagrancy Act sanctioned) did much to stem their numbers. Expelled from the city Liberties, they still had a refuge in places like Holloway from which they could daily 'glide... into the streets of Bath', as one observer put it, and exhibit their sores and maimed limbs to public gaze - and this notwithstanding the fact that the Hospital Act of 1738 required the Bathforum justices to commit vagrants found within five miles of Bath to hard labour at Shepton. By the 1780s and 1790s any expressions of pity seemed lost in the general complaint about the 'swarms' of beggars, idle and unprofitable, who 'infest' the streets and 'besiege our doors' - a problem that the war with France only aggravated and which the authorities seemed powerless to combat.

Prostitution was also endemic. A spa whose very waters were thought to promote fertility offered a splendid cloak for erotic adventure and a ready market in sex. Pimps and prostitutes operated wherever visitors resorted, at lodgings, pleasure gardens, theatre, assembly rooms, even the promenades and the riverside meadows - as Parson Woodforde discovered in 1779 (giving two teenage prostitutes he encountered in the fields a shilling and 'some good advice'). In 1785 'disorderly women' haunted the Parades every night, quarrelling, blaspheming and generally giving offence. Those working from pubs and brothels made easier targets for the magistrates in their occasional raids on premises, sometimes after a tip-off. That was how in 1727 they had convicted one Bath couple 'of keeping a bad House of Repute, and procuring of Young Women to be debauch'd'. The punishment in this case was a stint in the pillory, but inconsistencies in sentencing perhaps reflected the authorities' dilemma on how to treat prostitution. Women seized from a brothel in 1758 were sent to gaol, whereas in 1771 two New King Street madams were merely bound over and forced to move house. A 'nest of prostitutes' who had been pestering the Cross Bath area around 1784 were dispersed either to their home parishes or the Shepton Bridewell, but nearly sixty streetwalkers picked up in 1799 during a general sweep suffered only detention overnight. The belief that gaoling such women served no useful purpose had gained enough ground by 1805 to encourage local reformers to found an asylum for contrite prostitutes, the Bath Penitentiary.

Reform - this time of poor children - was similarly the object of the Sunday Schools, because the ragged urchins of Bath were another affront to the spa's image as they roamed the streets, begging, swearing, fighting, picking over rubbish heaps, shrilly hawking sand from house to house. Standards of public decency were rising, and people increasingly complained about noise, smells, the presence of pigsties and slaughterhouses, unswept streets (especially in slummier districts like Avon Street), obstructed pavements, dangerous horse traffic, disorderly alehouses, and many other nuisances which the Corporation and Bath Commissioners now felt obliged to attend to. The mass of detail in the Walcot and Bathwick Improvement Acts

(1793 and 1801), which Bath itself adopted in 1814, is an index of how many activities now came under official ban, from nude bathing in the river to the emptying of privies except at dead of night. In another controlling measure, successive Mayors shut down many gin-shops and small alehouses, so that the total of all licensed premises reduced from 176 in 1781 to around a 100 in 1789. Pub closing time (11p.m.) was also being rigorously enforced by 1800.

••• See also **Charities**; **Parish Administration**; **Police**; **Poorhouses**; **Public Health**.

Society of Guardians

The belief in lost golden ages is usually illusory, but the later Georgians held a strong belief that Bath before c.1740 had been relatively crime-free - 'a Place of Security even when our Doors were open'. By 1752, though, it seemed evident that theft certainly was a growing menace, only to be deterred by the absolute certainty of prosecution. The difficulty was that, even when offenders were caught, their victims often jibbed at laying charges because of the cost and trouble of attending trial at the distant county courts. To encourage bringing actions therefore, a private subscription was proposed: participants would each pay five shillings to raise a fund for employing an attorney and prosecuting thieves and receivers. This attempt of 1752 to establish a mutual protection society was the germ of the far more prominent Bath Society of Guardians of the 1780s onwards. Between those dates the subscription kept going, with periodic replenishment of the prosecutions fund (as in both 1764 and 1774 after public meetings at the Guildhall). A more active campaign to extend the Society's influence and increase its income began in 1783. Under its energetic secretary, William Meyler, the number of annual subscribers rose in six years to 414, though a mere seven of these lived in the supposedly 'more exposed' suburbs outside the city liberties and thus paid a higher subscription of 7s.6d. The aim of protecting subscribers' property and persons 'from Felons, Forgers, Receivers of Stolen Goods, Swindlers, Highwaymen, &c.' was primarily achieved by paying witnesses' expenses, at a rate of half-a-guinea per day, when they testified at the Somerset Assizes, by rewarding citizens and officers who helped make arrests, and by advertising at large the heavy punishments meted out to those convicted, notably whipping, imprisonment and transportation. Long excluded from the Society's protection, however, were nurseries and gardens not immediately adjacent to subscribers' own houses, so the whole scheme had to be paralleled by a second one run by the local Gardeners' Society to combat robberies from small-holdings, orchards, greenhouses, and the like. Another drawback was that only a minority of tradespeople and householders belonged to the Society of Guardians. The rest were as reluctant to prosecute as ever, not just out of 'false lenity' as the *Bath Herald* claimed but because of the sheer expense and hassle involved. But of course it meant, the *Chronicle* regretted in 1800, that 'many notorious thieves have escaped punishment'. It also increased pressure for a court empowered to try serious cases on the spot in Bath.

Somerset Assizes and Sessions

The fact that the county courts *alone* could try criminal and serious civil cases to do with Bath, even trifling cases of petty larceny, was a long-standing grudge, especially since the proceedings took place at the rather far-off venues of Wells, Taunton and Bridgwater. A few Assizes had been held at the spa in the 1600s, but efforts to include Bath on the regular circuit always foundered on the rock of county opposition. The result was that - until the Society of Guardians came into being - Bathonians would often refuse to press charges. At their Quarter Sessions the Somerset justices heard middle-level offences such as serious debt, persistent vagrancy, brothel-keeping, and petty larceny, but left capital cases to the circuit judges. Sessions required properly empanelled grand and petty juries, but the full judicial hierarchy rarely appeared and as a rule just a handful of county J.P.s presided. Bath officials attended as required to give evidence, and the Mayor usually attended the January Sessions in person to take his oaths of office (before the J.P.s sitting privately) - even though legal opinion in 1798 held that the Bath Quarter Sessions would have served equally well. The twice-yearly Somerset Assizes at which the two circuit judges sat with county magnates were rather more ceremonious affairs. Bath Mayors regularly attended (or sent apologies if they could not), as did the Town Clerk and sometimes other Corporation representatives - expeditions demanding hire of horses and carriages, refreshments en route, and perhaps the ferrying of witnesses and overnight accommodation. The actual trials were conducted at some speed in double sessions - a Crown court for criminal cases and a *nisi prius* court for civil actions. Given the range of statutory capital crimes, juries inclined to leniency. In the end only occasional Bath offenders faced the gallows, but not a few were transported, whipped, or sentenced to hard labour and irons in unwholesome gaols.

••• See also **Gaols (County)**; **Society of Guardians**.

Street Lighting

Pre-Georgian Bath was very dimly lit at night, and despite the ten oil lamps specially purchased for Queen Anne's visit in 1702, visitors still complained that the city was not 'sufficiently enlightened'. These words are taken from the Bath Act of 1707 which for the first time imposed a statutory duty on householders to hang out a lantern themselves or else pay a rate towards the municipal street lamps. Eventually all the lighting would come under appointed contractors, but some citizens, especially lodging-house keepers, supplied private candle lanterns as late as the 1760s. Adequate illumination helped deter crime, and the Act of 1739 prescribed specific penalties for extinguishing or damaging lamps. Mostly oil-burning and housed in flint-glass globes, they had to be individually lit and doused at prescribed hours and needed frequent maintenance, tasks the contractors sometimes fell down on. Householders too could be reluctant to pay their lighting rates, the very reason John Wood II removed all the Walcot parish lamps in winter 1755-6. While central Bath seemed quite well illuminated compared with other towns, people might still carry horn lanterns or even 'links' (flaming torches) on moonless nights, and sedan chairs were required to be accompanied by lights. From 1766 the regulation of lighting came under the new body of Bath Commissioners who quickly set to work standardising, repositioning, and boosting the number of lamps. All the lighting equipment belonged to the Commissioners who tendered with local tinsmiths and ironmongers to produce lamps according to a set pattern. In due course experiments were made with new designs - better forms of wick, convex reflectors, lamp chimneys - as well as with the new Argand lamps from Birmingham - so that by 1800 Bath seemed conspicuously well illuminated, sunset to sunrise, autumn round to spring, with just half-lighting in the out-of-season summer months. Only with the arrival of brighter, more manageable gas lighting in 1819 would it become obvious that oil lamps had not been such effective illuminants after all.

Streets and Highways see Scavenging; Sewerage; Street Lighting; Traffic Control; Turnpike Trusts

Supervisors

Every year the Corporation formally nominated pairs of minor officials as embryonic trading standards inspectors - two Supervisors of Flesh and Fish (who respectively oversaw the Shambles and the Fish Market), two of Leather, and two of Ale (also termed Ale Tasters). Another pair, the Supervisors of Bounds, presumably checked for encroachments affecting parish and city boundaries including those of the Common. All eight received just a guinea a year each for their trouble, so the duties must have been light enough. Only occasionally was there mention of tainted commodities (e.g. unfit meat, rotten fish) being seized and burnt, while inspection of bread and dairy produce, or of weights and measures themselves, seems to have fallen to the Mayor's and Bailiffs' officers. Some Supervisors held their job for many years, most notably the Cottle family who from 1720 onwards dominated one of the Leather Supervisors' posts.

Surveyor see City Surveyor

Swans

The city accounts for 1710-11 record a payment for 'taking up' the swans, but only from the 1760s is it clear that the Corporation deliberately maintained these uniquely royal birds 'as an Ornament to the River'. A stern reminder went out in 1763, after one had been maliciously injured, that to kill a swan was a felony and that even to purloin the eggs merited imprisonment. On several occasions between 1768 and 1774 the Chamber reimbursed people for feeding the swans in hard weather, and once in 1783 for returning a stray. This suggests Bath might have owned its own identifying swan mark, as several other cities did, but no such mark is officially recorded.

Tithingmen see Parish Administration; Police

Town Clerk

Normally elected by the Council from among the city's leading attorneys, the Town Clerk was Bath's official solicitor and its chief legal adviser next to the Recorder. His numerous duties, which can have left little time for private legal practice, included frequent attendance at sittings of the magistrates. He or a deputy took minutes at Council meetings, though not formally a member, and he was expected to attend the main quarterly meetings in person and to witness oathtaking. He acted as clerk of the peace, prothonotary of the Court of Record, aide to the Mayor sitting as coroner, steward of the manor (and hence of the Court Leet), deputy to the Bailiffs, keeper of official records, and clerk and treasurer to the Turnpike Trust. Not only did he attend Assizes, he often enough journeyed to London on Corporation business. Thus in 1706 and 1708 Smith spent 15 weeks there, defending city's rights and promoting the first improvement Bill, and his successors did much the same - none more so than Jefferys over the protracted suit with St Michael's parish. Like the Recorder the Town Clerk received for most of the period only a token £4 honorarium, and even that was not automatically paid, since the Town Clerk in 1794 needed to claim over sixteen years' arrears. Though his salary jumped in 1793 to £50 in recognition of extra work, it was still not a large sum when he had to employ in his office a deputy, and a clerk or two besides, to copy endless documents, transcribe rent rolls, and keep the Chamberlain's accounts. He was of course far from out of pocket, being entitled to fees and expenses (for routine clerical services, stationery, conveyancing, court work) and costs when away on Corporation duties. His deputy would normally be a junior solicitor who sometimes succeeded to the full post, as Clutterbuck did after a long probation under Robarts, Jefferys under Clutterbuck, and Philip George under Jefferys. From the late 1780s until his promotion in 1800 George seems to have been shouldering most of the routine work with the help of a changing staff of junior employees. Deputy Town Clerks too received fees according to a set scale, e.g. (in 1776) 1s. for a summons, 2s. for an arrest warrant, 5s. for enrolling an apprentice, 5s.6d. for admitting a freeman.

Surprisingly Town Clerks were not required to be freemen themselves. To be versed in law, sound at arguing a case, assiduous in serving writs, skilled in drawing up documents, these were the qualities needed. The Council often entrusted the Town Clerk with specific commissions - to frame new bylaws, draft petitions, prosecute illegal traders, handle sales of property, recover rent arrears, issue public notices, consult with the Recorder, defend municipal privileges, or lobby Parliament. In 1738 it was Robarts who made the Corporation's complimentary speech to the Prince of Wales, and in 1788 Jefferys who addressed the King at Cheltenham. When the Town Clerk had so much behind-the-scenes influence, his reputation for probity, discretion and impartiality had to be unblemished. Jacob Smith was abruptly replaced by William Webb in 1704 yet the dismissal reflected not on him but on William Chapman, Mayor at the time of his contested election, and in due course he was re-elected. Lewis Clutterbuck won respect for his unforced resignation from the Council on election to the Town Clerkship, and his successor Jefferys was described in 1782 as learned in law, moderate in fees, and incorruptibly honest.

••• **List of Town Clerks 1700-1800**: *John Bushell 1679-1702; Jacob Smith 1702-04 and 1706-33; William Webb 1704-06; Randolph*

*Webb 1733-38; Richard Robarts 1738-57; Lewis Clutterbuck 1757-76;
John Jefferys 1776-1800; Philip George 1800-*

Town Common

In 1619, following a legal dispute between the citizens of Bath and the landlord of Walcot, the citizens had been awarded a large tract of freehold pasture on the north-west side of the city, to be known as Bath Common and managed by the Corporation for the burgesses' benefit. In practice this was done by renting it out to the best bidder, appointing Corporation overseers, and sharing the annual profits among the freemen. For the next two centuries the land was used mainly for fattening cattle and sheep, dairying, haymaking, dumping town waste (including nightsoil from cesspits), and stone and gravel quarrying. In 1699 the Corporation encroached on the Common in order to lay out a riding area where the visiting gentry could take the air. The farm itself was let for increasingly longer terms (up to 14 years) at annual rents rising from around £120 in 1700 to £180 by 1740, £230 by 1792, and £500 in the 1830s. It was bounded by stone walls and contained a substantial farm- and dairy-house (built 1742-56), but by the 1780s the Common's agricultural future was coming into question. Around 1781 the Corporation yielded to demands for gravel for private garden walks and allowed individuals to extract it. In 1784 John Symons, himself a Councilman, put forward a plan to landscape the lower Common with clumps of trees and to create a broad, tree-lined gravel walk between the farmhouse and Weston Lane, paid for by public subscription. This was rejected, but pressure to develop such a desirable site increased as Marlborough Buildings, St James's Square and new properties on Sion Hill spread along its eastern and northern margins. A cold bath was built near the farm, developers illegally diverted springs, and soon there was talk of making a reservoir on the upper Common.

Bath was now in a hectic phase of growth, with new streets and buildings emerging everywhere on greenfield sites whose values rocketed accordingly. The freemen spotted their opportunity, claiming that the Common, which they considered theirs, would be worth £7000-£8000 a year if suitably exploited. Twice in 1789 they petitioned the Mayor, but finding the Corporation evasive and slow even to produce the full accounts, the freemen's committee embarked in 1791 on a Chancery suit to exert pressure. Their argument was simple. There was a duty on the Corporation, as trustees, to improve their property. Against this the Corporation argued that the Common had been awarded to *all* Bath residents, not merely the freemen, and that many householders in fact opposed development. In any case the Recorder, Earl Camden, believed a fresh local Act of Parliament would be needed, which the Corporation were disinclined to promote. As to the accounts, the Chamberlain produced disheartening figures. Between 1777 and 1791 the expenses had virtually matched the receipts, leaving a balance of only £6-19s. By 1793 it appeared the promoters were no further forward and the ensuing economic slump dampened any hopes of building on the Common in the short term. Nonetheless in 1804 the freemen were again badgering the Corporation for a Bill, and the dream of capitalising on the Common continued to agitate local politics for years to come, only to fade in 1830 with the laying out of Royal Victoria Park.

Town Crier

Elected annually by the Council, the Town Crier doubled in the earlier eighteenth century as Beadle, a uniformed servant of the Mayor and Justices. His original job was to help preserve the peace, attend court sessions, execute warrants, serve summonses, and, as his title suggests, proclaim important public news at set places in the city - the succession of George III in 1760, for example, being cried at five points (Guildhall, Queen Square, twice in Stall Street, Parades) from temporary platforms covered with scarlet cloth. Traditionally the Crier also removed vagrants and beggars on the magistrates' orders, which might involve whipping them out of town. About 1737, on the appointment of a new man to the post, many of the Beadle's duties were hived off and given to separate officers. The Crier then took on duties to do with the provisions market and, until superseded in 1767 by a Deputy Clerk of the Market, he hired out standings on behalf of the Bailiffs, collected fees, and rang the market bell to signal the hours of trading. After 1767 he was responsible for keeping the Guildhall area clean and swept, and was allowed four guineas a year for mops, brushes, soap and sand, and sometimes extra for washing the Guildhall linen. He still wore Corporation livery and occasionally cried local news about the streets (e.g. notices to the freemen to collect their dividends). He also retained his policing role - an elegy on Thomas Clarke recalls him pursuing rogues through the dark streets with the resounding cry 'Beware!'. Basic accommodation probably went with the job, but the post was not lucrative and some Criers served many years yet still died poor. Indeed the salary even went down - from about £18 in 1774 to £10 by 1801, at which point it was suddenly uprated to £20.

••• See also **Beadles.**

••• **List of Town Criers 1700-1800**: *Thomas Tovey 1696-1710; John Wornell 1710-21; John Allen 1721-37; Richard Bishop 1737-47 (and his widow 1747-8); Robert Woodruff 1748-56; Thomas Dawson 1756-75; Thomas Kircum 1775-96; Thomas Clarke 1796- .*

Town Hall see **Guildhall**

Trade Companies

Stimulated by the new vogue for water-drinking, spa custom was quickening by the 1680s and inevitably tempted outsiders of many sorts to try their luck at Bath. The Corporation's natural reaction was to take a strong line in defence of the freemen's interests, first by invoking the customary rules against interlopers, and second by helping to revive the Companies - i.e. the old craft guilds or trading monopolies. Possibly only the Merchant Tailors, the Shoemakers - the two dominant trades in point of numbers - and the Weavers guilds had survived the Civil War and Commonwealth intact, but others were showing signs of life. The Corporation approved the constitutions of the Bakers (1681) and the Haberdashers & Feltmakers (1687), and a Council minute of 1683 refers to a society of Joiners and Carvers. Nevertheless, a mere three Companies took part in the Guy Fawkes and other processions around 1700, when each organisation received five shillings per event from the city purse. Of these the Merchant Tailors, the senior organisation, had a membership of almost forty master tailors who operated a restrictive-practice cartel that controlled apprenticeships, fixed prices and journeymen's wages, had powers to fine or sue, and attempted to monopolise the whole trade of tailoring.

Even so, despite the Council's repeated threats that 'unqualified' traders would be prosecuted, they refused to be deterred. By 1726 the Corporation was frankly admitting that the freemen's privileges had often been infringed by strangers who set up shops but escaped most of the charges and duties laid on other citizens. A tougher policy was promised with a £5 fine for every offence, but in practice this was hard to enforce given that the franchise (the freedom rights) did not stem from the Charter but rested solely on ancient precedent. Court actions brought in 1731 depended on the weighty support of the Recorder and the Solicitor-General himself, and five years later the bylaws against interlopers still seemed 'ineffectual'. Struggling for dominance (and competing with tailors living in the suburbs outside the Liberties), 54 Merchant Tailors agreed in 1734 on more vigorous action to bar non-freemen, with the result that five different tailors were eventually prosecuted. The master apothecaries threatened similar action in 1746, and the Corporation finally launched a major campaign in 1751 to back the freemen and revitalise the Companies. Shopkeepers and others without trading rights (always excepting market traders to whom the freedom rules did not apply) were given until April 1752 to buy their freedom or face court proceedings, and in May the Companies paraded for the first time - with painted banners and music - in the Corporation's grand Restoration Day procession. Only two of the nine Companies on show - Merchant Tailors and Shoemakers - could boast an unbroken tradition. The old Weavers Company had become defunct c.1744, and the other seven had just been refounded - Masons, Carpenters and Joiners, Tilers and Plasterers, Bakers, Barbers and Wigmakers, Grocers and Chandlers, and Mercers and Drapers.

These highly visible expressions of town-and-trade solidarity continued - the Companies being rewarded with a guinea for every appearance (e.g. each 5 November and 29 June) and double that at the 1761 Coronation. The new hardline policy brought the Chamber considerable extra revenue from purchased freedoms and led to a surge in apprenticeship enrolments, but legally the Corporation occupied shaky ground. In 1753 the prosecution of a non-freeman, the well-known perfumer Duperré, had been attacked in a libellous pamphlet, and the Mayor and his colleagues searched the archives in vain for evidence to support their position. The real test began in 1759 as the Merchant Tailors embarked on a long-drawn-out case against a particular tailor, William Glazby, for practising without being free and for refusing to pay fines. The eventual judgment in 1765 that only the Corporation might bring such prosecutions undermined the whole idea that the Companies had a primary right to stifle competition. But of course the Corporation could not effectively prosecute either - for lack of proof that the freemen enjoyed a unique privilege to trade. The Glazby affair thus opened the way to an economic free-for-all, and the subsequent dissolution of the Companies (though the Merchant Tailors lingered on awhile) may have led to a worsening of labour relations in each trade.

••• See also **Apprentices**; **Freemen**; **Friendly Societies**; **Journeymen**; **Master Tradesmen**.

Trade Unions see Journeymen

Traffic Control

Narrow-streeted central Bath, where most of the coaching inns stood, was ill-suited to the density of horses and horse-drawn vehicles that the growing spa attracted. The lack of a direct north-south route simply aggravated matters, since traffic between Walcot Street/Broad Street and Stall Street/Bath Bridge had to negotiate an often cluttered Marketplace and a sharp change of direction through constricted Cheap Street. The creation of Milsom Street in the 1760s made little difference, the *Bear* inn still blocking the way south. Well aware of the worsening congestion, noise, and disturbance, the Corporation had demolished the three obstructive gateways in 1754-5, and by the 1757 Improvement Act forced laden coal wagons to avoid the city centre at night and go via Borough Walls instead. Although horse traffic of any sort tended to pulverise pitched road surfaces, some of the turnpike legislation could at least be used to deter the worst culprits - heavy, narrow-wheeled wagons and carts. The Bath Act of 1766 reinforced these rules and gave the Bath Commissioners powers to order the removal or impounding of vehicles causing obstruction. One reason for building the vegetable market in 1762-3 had been to clear the Marketplace of traders' baskets and so 'give Room for Carriages to stand and turn'. Pulling down the old Guildhall in 1777 removed another bottleneck, but made the lower Marketplace into a permanent carriage park - an all-too-tempting spot (according to a shopkeepers' complaint in 1799) for 'Medical Gentlemen' to leave their obstructive vehicles. Other road schemes too opened up the centre, especially the bypass from Southgate to Queen Square (1776), Bath Street (1790-4) and York Street (from 1796). The belated widening of Bath's most accident-prone thoroughfare, Cheap Street, in the 1790s improved traffic flow, but still left scope for dangerous driving (see *Northanger Abbey* ch.7). However, driving animals 'furiously' had already become a statutory offence in the Walcot Act of 1793, and the subsequent

Bathwick Act also laid down special rules for coal carts travelling into Bath from Sydney wharf. In another attempt to minimise disturbance the magistrates allowed the churchwardens at St Michael's to chain off Green Street for nearly two hours during Sunday morning service. Otherwise only in the matter of sedan chairs (and, potentially, hackney cabs), where they had licensing powers, could they assert direct control of traffic.

••• See also **Pitching and Paving**; **Sedan Chairmen**.

Turnkey see **Gaoler**

Turnpike Trusts

Named after the toll barriers they erected across highways, turnpike trusts gradually took over the country's road network from parish administration by means of hundreds of local Acts of Parliament which set them up and developed their powers. The Bath Act of 1707, one of the earliest, did double duty in fact, for it authorised various street improvements within the city as well as the turnpiking of the 'very Ruinous and Impassable' roads that led to it. By the 1760s the initial 12½ miles under the Bath Turnpike Trust had expanded in stages to nearly 50 miles and had linked up with other turnpike systems. The earlier legislation placed the Trust in the hands of 'Seven or more... Justices' who could appoint surveyors and toll collectors and also raise capital (mortgage-fashion) on the security of toll profits. This fairly simple administration, in which one of the current Bath J.P.s served as a Commissioner with six colleagues from Somerset, Wiltshire and Gloucestershire, prevailed until the radical overhaul of 1757 which transformed the Trust into a deed-holding body financed by some 400 investors. At this date the capital fund amounted to £12,000, while tolls levied on coaches, wagons, horses and livestock yielded c.£1200 per annum. Both sums were set to rise significantly by the 1790s - capital to £25,000 and revenue to over £7000. Income from the most profitable route, the great London Road, had been endangered in the early 1770s by Pulteney's plan for a turnpike bypass through Bathwick, which the Corporation and the Trust Commissioners successfully resisted. Their interests were indeed so entwined that there was rarely friction until the Corporation's Bill of 1789 to finance city improvements by raising turnpike tolls, a move the Trust opposed in vain. The city cooperated on renewals of the relevant Turnpike Acts, granted land for road widening, and permitted its Town Clerk to serve as clerk and treasurer to the Trust - which often met at the Guildhall. In return, at no cost to itself, it saw the roads converging on Bath gradually improve. Cutting journey times for people and goods undoubtedly stimulated tourism and economic growth generally, and by 1784 the vital London route had already improved to such an extent that the new mail coaches could reach the capital in thirteen hours.

Vagrants see Social Problems

Vestries see Parish Administration

Voluntary Associations

Philanthropic institutions such as the General Hospital, City Infirmary, Bluecoats School and the Sunday Schools were pre-eminent examples of bodies founded by groups of individuals for what they saw as some public good. These high-status organisations, smiled on by the city fathers, publicised in the guidebooks, supported by church collections and charity concerts, were only the best-known of many voluntary associations which enjoyed varying degrees of official backing. Some acted under the banner of law and order. The Society of Guardians (1752 in its origins) and the Committee on Forestallers (c.1765-c.1770) both existed primarily to raise funds to bring court prosecutions. More obviously philanthropic were bodies such as the Bath branch of the Thatched House Society for the relief of gaoled debtors (active by 1786), the Strangers' Friend Society (started by Wesleyan Methodists in 1790) to help the destitute without parish support, and the Bath Provisions Society which supplied soup, cheap foodstuffs and coal to Bath's hungry poor in 1795-6 and 1799-1801. The Shopkeepers' Committee (1785-9) demanding repeal of the Shops' Act, and - in the heated 1790s - the local Anti-Slavetrade campaigners, the Parliamentary reform groups, and the reactionary Loyalist Association, all took a more political line. Even the Concerts Committee and the early Bath & West Agricultural Society (founded 1777) regarded themselves as public benefactors, the former in supporting the Pump Room concerts as a general amenity, the latter in improving farm practice and encouraging useful inventions.

•••   See also **Freemasons**; **Friendly Societies**; **Infirmaries**; **Loyalist Association**; **Society of Guardians**.

Volunteers see **Militias and Volunteers**

Waits

More often called the 'City Music' than 'Waits', this was the town wind band, four to five players in all. Their main employment in the season had always been serenading visitors - at their lodgings, at the Cross Bath, in Gravel Walks - and otherwise playing at private events. Needing a larger mixed orchestra (with strings) and more control, Beau Nash hired performers from London to play at the new Pump and Assembly Rooms rather than the Waits - who apparently bore him no grudge since fifty years later they marched alongside the Pump Room musicians in Nash's funeral cortège. The Corporation customarily employed the Waits whenever they required music (e.g. on Ascension Day) and from 1733 salaried them as the City Music to perform at the October mayor-making and other civic events. Otherwise the band kept up their freelance activities, undeterred by the magistrates' attempts (especially in 1774-5) to stop them pestering visitors on threat of being struck off the city payroll. In the 1790s they were still receiving their guinea a year each, with special payments for extra duties like 'processioning', at the same time as newly arrived visitors were being advised not to reward their unsanctioned lodging-house recitals.

Walcot

Bath's northern boundary bisected the parish, dividing it unequally into Inner Walcot (under borough jurisdiction) and the much larger Outer Walcot (under the county division of Bathforum). This hardly mattered as long as the village core near St Swithin's remained small and isolated, but by c.1770 streets and buildings were invading across the divide and soon enfolding old Walcot within the new upper town. The administrative anomalies quickly became obvious, for none of the fashionable new developments - stretching from St James's Square and upper Lansdown to Lambridge - enjoyed Bath's statutory provisions for policing, street-lighting, chair-licensing, etc., or had any equivalent of the Bath Commissioners. By late 1791 Bath Council seemed poised to apply to Parliament for an extension of boundaries that would bring Outer Walcot into the fold, but fifteen months later the plan had stalled. If one reason was the current preoccupation with rebuilding central

Bath, then it was deeply ironic because it was Walcot's effect in siphoning off trade from the lower town that made the latter's revitalisation necessary. The Corporation did agree to license sedans for Walcot and it accepted the parishioners' right to proceed independently, but paid nothing towards the costs of the highly detailed Walcot Act obtained in 1793. This named a governing board of thirty Commissioners, many of whom, like William Pulteney, were currently active in promoting new developments. All of them fulfilled the substantial property qualification laid down in the Act and were empowered to act as J.P.s., but their remit covered only public services, policing, and the like, leaving other areas of administration (e.g. Poor Law matters) to the parish Vestry. It would be for the Commissioners, though, to resolve the dispute between the Corporation and the Walcot Highways Surveyor in 1795 over the right to quarry stone from the Town Common. This was another grey area, but the Corporation had legal claim to be sole trustee of the Common on behalf of the Bath freemen, despite the fact that the land lay wholly in Walcot parish and much of it not subject to the city justices. The rest of Walcot belonged to the Manor and a limited number of freeholders. A map of 1740 shows a jigsaw pattern of small enclosed fields, whose gradual release in building plots over the next century virtually dictated how Walcot got built. By 1800 it was already enormously rich in real estate and Bath's most populous parish.

••• See also **Liberties of Bath**; **Poorhouses**; **Private Estates**; **Water Supply**.

••• **List of Lords of Walcot Manor**: *Robert Gay 1699-1737; Margaret Garrard 1737-65; Sir Benet Garrard 1765-7; Sir Peter Rivers Gay 1767-90; Sir Thomas Rivers Gay 1790-1805.*

••• **List of Rectors of Walcot**: *Joseph Dresser 1688-1707; William Heath 1707-21; Marcus Hall 1721-26; Robert Chapman 1726-28; James Sparrow 1728-74; John Sibley 1774-1815.*

Water Supply

Hot waters made Bath, but plain drinking water was needed too. Cold springs emerged at many places in the surrounding hills, though often on private land. Traditionally the Corporation had rights to two supplies, the 'upper' water from Beacon Hill and the 'lower' or St James's water from Beechen Cliff, and neither came strictly free. The grant of the upper water in 1552 included an obligation to support an almshouse and a grammar school, while exploitation of the lower water meant paying rent to the owners of Beechen Cliff (i.e. the almshouse at Bruton) and allowing a modest flow to residents in Holloway and to the future Kingston Estate. Both waters originally fed public fountains or 'conduits' at strategic points in the city. The upper water descended first in an open channel, and then through elmwood or lead pipes branching off to the various ornamental conduits in Walcot Street (Cornwell), Broad Street, outside St Michael's, the Marketplace (both St Mary's and the Abbey conduits), and at the top of Stall Street. In the same way the lower water, piped over Bath bridge, supplied the St James's conduit at Southgate - and later, it seems, the Stall Street conduit. But gradually, as the architect John Wood lamented, all the handsome conduits were replaced by simple taps on nearby walls where they caused less obstruction. For example St Mary's conduit, four-sided, domed and pinnacled, was lost this way in 1722.

Collecting every drop of water for household needs from a public fountain was of course inconvenient, so increasingly from the later 1600s wealthier residents paid a water rate to have pipes laid off the mains to their own houses. Though it was profitable for the Corporation to grant these private 'feathers of water', it worried about the effect on the supply and as early as 1731 employed an inspector to check on wastage. The fact that houses were 'very ill supply'd' led to fresh Corporation activity from the mid-1740s. River water was pumped into a reservoir that could be tapped for purposes such as street cleansing and fire-fighting. On the upper water the leaky stone culvert and cisterns were improved and the pipes widened, and with some difficulty the city repossessed the so-called 'waste' from the lower water which had been hitherto rented out. It was still not enough and in the 1750/1760s the focus switched to bringing more water from Beechen Cliff. This involved building a reservoir in 1756-7 on land owned by one of the Corporation (E.B. Collibee), laying a new pipe down Holloway road, negotiating with Bruton and Kingston interests, and finally obtaining Parliamentary approval in the Act of 1766. Despite having to deliver water to the Kingston estate equivalent to the flow of a $1^1/4''$ pipe for four hours a day, the Corporation was now in a position to increase supplies to private properties at rentals of ten shillings a year upwards, with stopcocks fitted to cut off the water for non-payment. An official called the turncock controlled the flow to different districts at specified hours, most houses having tanks capable of storing two hogheads (i.e. over 100 gallons) or more. Supplies improved yet again after 1769 thanks to the Pulteney Bridge Act. This granted municipal use of three springs rising on the Bathwick estate - the 'Castle water' - and the construction of a 100'-long reservoir in a field called Under Egypt.

Private building developments created the greatest demand for water. In the late 1750s the Circus scheme caused considerable friction as the younger John Wood and his builders bargained with landowners, jockeyed with rivals, and surveyed possible springs and aqueduct routes from as far off as Weston as well as nearer sources under Beacon Hill or close to the High Common. Unless the reservoir planned for the centre of the Circus succeeded, the whole building project would have been in jeopardy. In the end the springs at the north-east side of the Common produced enough to supply most of the Woods' upper town including Queen Square and Royal Crescent. But disputes over water inevitably recurred, above all during the speculative building boom around 1790. The city's upper water became contentious once more when the surgeon John Symons, himself a Council member, constructed a new, larger reservoir under Beacon Hill in connection with his Camden Crescent development. This led to a financial wrangle with the Corporation and years later to the Walcot estate winning its case for a half share in the Beacon Hill supply. The respective projectors of Lansdown Crescent in 1791 and of St James's Square in 1794 had both to be threatened with prosecution for diverting streams, and in 1792 the Corporation protested to the Pulteneys that Thomas Baldwin had been interfering with the Castle springs in order to supply Bathwick. What with these and other difficulties, such as wilful damage to the waterworks, the Corporation (and its Water Committee) remained acutely concerned about this staple public service which it now shared with a growing number of private water companies. But at least the sources were still fairly safe. Few people were supplied by wells or from the Avon (though at least one brewery used river water), and even poorer citizens without their own domestic supply had access to fresh spring water at the open taps. It was much later, in Victorian Bath, that water contamination and public health become a major issue.

••• See also **Baths and Pump Rooms**; **Pumper**; **Sewerage**.

Weighing Engine

From 1763 a £70 weighbridge, sturdy enough to weigh a loaded wagon, stood prominently in Sawclose. With a full-time attendant in John Sherborne (and subsequently his widow) this soon proved a profitable venture. Despite the costs of maintenance, lamps, rates, and complete renewal twice (1774 and 1789), the overall income from weighing coal and farm vehicles increasingly boosted the Chamberlain's accounts - from c.£75 per annum c.1765 to over £200 by 1800.

Weights and Measures

Some commodities sold in special quantities - say, a firkin of butter (56lbs) or a stone of fish (8lbs), and it appears Bath measured corn by a local 9-gallon bushel until as late as 1792 when it adopted the Winchester 8-gallon rule. Otherwise it largely accepted national norms, and the Guildhall and market held various official weights and measures on which to standardise local practice. In 1742, already equipped with bushel, peck, quart and pint measures, the Corporation sent to London for others. It had long provided market scales for weighing ordinary produce as a public check on traders, and in 1762 ordered extra scales to weigh skins, leather and tallow. In 1787 the Guildhall possessed 'very exact' money scales for weighing guineas etc., a necessary tool when coin-clipping was common. Measuring vessels for selling milk had to be certified and stamped at the Guildhall, but hawkers of fruit and vegetables used all sorts of containers not easy to check. Even shop scales and market steelyards were suspect, as the Mayor's officers found on their periodic swoops.

In 1795 they confiscated many faulty greengrocers' measures, and in 1796 discovered defective weights at 55 different shops. Reports of underweight butter being seized (50 lbs of it from a single dealer) were common at this period - despite advice given to the Mayor in 1783 that summary seizures of this kind had no legal warrant and that cheating traders must be tried first at Bath Quarter Sessions.

The city owned two other standards. One was a measuring wheel, presumably the survey tool employed to determine distances between various key points in and about the city. Tables of measured distances were printed in Bath guidebooks and used to calculate sedan chair fares. An equally practical but much more venerated instrument was the Tompion timepiece, an accurate equation clock delivered to the Corporation c.1709. Stationed in the Pump Room and cared for by a succession of local clockmakers (paid a guinea or so a year for their trouble), this clock announced official Bath time to generations of residents and visitors who set their watches by it. Its accompanying sundial may have been fixed for a time on the outside wall overlooking the King's Bath.

••• See also **Assize of Bread**; **Weighing Engine**.

Widcombe see Lyncombe and Widcombe

Workhouses see Bridewell; Poorhouses

A Note on Sources

This book is primarily based on original documents in Bath Record Office and Bath Central Library, whose staff have done much finding and carrying on my behalf and to whom I am most grateful. These sources are listed below together with a selection from the secondary material consulted. Particularly valuable have been the Minutes of Bath Council Meetings, the Chamberlain's Accounts, and files of local newspapers, each one a treasure-house for any student of Georgian Bath.

<u>Bath Record Office</u>
  Alehouse Recognizances 1776-89
  Assize of Bread, 1767-81
  Avon Navigation Papers
  Bath City Council, Minutes of Meetings, 1680-1820
  Bath City Council, Report Book of Committees, 1794-1837
  Bath Commissioners' Minutes, 1766-82
  Bath Gaol, Box 1
  Bath Improvement Commissioners' Minutes, 1789-1832
  Bath Loyalist Association, Minute Book
  Business before the Mayor and Justices, 1776-79
  Chamberlain's Vouchers, various bundles
  City General Committee Memorandum Book, 1774-79
  Commons Account Book, 1693-1746
  Coroner's Examinations, 1776-1814
  Corporation versus St Michael's, boxes 1-2, 7
  Court of Quarter Sessions, Sessions Books, 1682-1724, 1724-43, 1743-76
  Court of Record, Court Books, 1756-71, 1776-1803; Writ Book 1757-76
  Court of Requests, Court Book 1785-88
  Excise Prosecutions, 1797-1811
  Freemen's Apprentices, 1706-76
  James, P.R., The Charters of the City of Bath, 2v. (typescript)
  Justices' Day Book, 1776-79
  Philip George Papers
  Property Deeds, various bundles
  Pulteney Estate Papers
  Register of Freemen, 1776-
  Town Clerk's Accounts, 1747-1807
  Walcot Police Commissioners' Minutes, 1793-1815
  Waterworks Miscellaneous, Bundles 2, 4

Bath City Library, etc
  Autograph Letters collection
  Bath Advertiser, 1755-60
  Bath Chronicle, 1760-1800
  Bath Herald, 1792-1800
  Bath Journal, 1744-1800
  Broadsides and Posters collection
  Farley's Bristol Newspaper, 1725-30 (Bristol Reference Library)
  Gloucester Journal, 1725-45 (Gloucester Reference Library)
  Shickle, C.W., A List of the Honorary Freemen, 1632-1911 (typescript)
  Shickle, C.W., St James's Parish, 'Accounts, Vestry Meetings, etc.
(typescript)
  Shickle, C.W., St John's Hospital, 'Accounts' (typescript)
  Shickle, C.W., St Peter & Paul's Parish and St James's Parish, Poor House
Committee Book, 1784-1812 (typescript)
  Walcot Estate Papers

Select list of other primary and secondary sources
  Acts of Parliament (as detailed in the entry under this heading in the book)
  Bath: the City Charter (Bath, J. Salmon, 1775)
  Binney, J.E.D., *British Public Finance and Administration, 1774-92*
(Oxford, 1958)
  Borsay, Anne, *Medicine and Charity in Georgian Bath* (Aldershot, 1999)
  Boyce, Benjamin, *The Benevolent Man... Ralph Allen of Bath*
(Cambridge, Mass., 1967)
  Buchanan, B.J., 'The evolution of the English Turnpike Trusts', *Economic History Review*, 2nd series, v.39 n.2 (1986)
  Cannon, John, 'Bath politics in the eighteenth century', *Proceedings of the Somerset Archaeological Soc*, v.105 (1961)
  Chapman, Mike, *An Historical Guide to the Ham and Southgate Area of Bath* (Bath, 1997)
  Clew, K.R., *The Kennet & Avon Canal*, 3rd ed. (Newton Abbot, 1985)
  Clews, Stephen, 'Banking in Bath in the reign of George III', *Bath History*, v.5 (1994)
  Commissioners of Corporation Reform for the City of Bath, *Report* (Bath, T. Corbould, 1835)
  Complete Parish Officer, 7th ed. (London, 1734)
  Fawcett, Trevor, 'Fires, fire-fighting and insurance in 18th-century Bath', *Notes & Queries for Somerset & Dorset*, v.34 (1997)
  Fawcett, Trevor, *Paving, Lighting, Cleansing... in Eighteenth-Century Bath* (Bath, 1994)

Gentleman, Merchant... and Debtor's Pocket Guide in Cases of Arrest (Bath, W. Gye, 1785)

Hembry, Phyllis, *The English Spa, 1560-1815* (London, 1990)

Historical Manuscripts Commission, *Reports* (various)

Manco, Jean, *The Spirit of Care* (Bath, 1998)

McIntyre, Sylvia, 'Bath: the rise of a resort town, 1660-1800' in *Country Towns in Pre-Industrial England*, ed. P. Clark (Leicester, 1981)

Namier, L. and Brooke, J., *The History of Parliament*, 3v. (London, 1964)

Neale, R.S., *Bath: a Social History 1680-1850* (London, 1981)

New Bath Guide (various eds.)

Norman, George, 'The masonic lodges of Bath', *Transactions of the Somerset Masters Lodge* no. 3746 (1920-3), *passim*

Oldfield, T.H.B., *An Entire... History... of the Boroughs of Great Britain*, 3v. (London, 1792)

Plans of the Sunday Schools and School of Industry... Bath (Bath, 1789)

Poole, Steve, 'Radicalism, loyalism and the "reign of terror" in Bath, 1792-1804', *Bath History* v.3 (1990)

Poulter, John, *The Discoveries of John Poulter, alias Baxter*, 6th ed. (Sherborne, 1763)

Somerset Assize Orders, 1629-40, ed. T.G. Barnes (Somerset Record Soc. v.65, Frome, 1959)

State of the Bath City Infirmary and Dispensary (Bath, R. Cruttwell, 1794)

Trial of Jane Leigh Perrot... at Taunton Assizes, reported by J. Pinchard (Taunton, 1800)

Warner, Richard, *Excursions from Bath* (Bath, 1801)

Warner, Richard, *An Historical and Descriptive Account of Bath and its Environs* (Bath, 1802)

Warner, Richard, *The History of Bath* (Bath, 1801)

Webb, Sidney and Beatrice, *English Local Government*, v.1-4, 6 (London, 1906-22)

Western, J.R., *The English Militia in the Eighteenth Century* (London, 1965)

Wood, John, *An Essay towards a Description of Bath*, 2v. (Bath, 1742-3); 2nd ed. (Bath, 1749)

Wroughton, John, *King Edward's School at Bath 1552-1982* (Bath, 1982)

VOICES OF EIGHTEENTH-CENTURY BATH
An Anthology of Contemporary Texts illustrating Events, Daily Life and Attitudes at Britain's Leading Georgian Spa

A new approach to the history of Bath letting the evidence speak for itself in the echoing voices of its former residents and visitors - voices captured here in hundreds of revealing and entertaining extracts from letters, diaries, newspapers, official records, and many other sources. This key anthology is arranged in eighteen sections, each with its own historical introduction: The developing townscape - Transport - Industry, Trade & Retailing - Spa Facilities & Treatments - Visitors - Lodgings - Food & Drink - Assemblies, Gambling, &c - Theatre & Music - Excursions & Healthy Exercise - Serious Interests - Education - Religion - Corporation, Politics, &c - Disorder, Crime & Punishment - Poverty - Loyalty & Royalty - Beau Nash & his Successors

Compiled by Trevor Fawcett

Bath, Ruton, 1995: 208 pp in A5: £9: ISBN 0-9526326-0-8

BATH ENTERTAIN'D
Amusements, Recreations and Gambling at the 18th-Century Spa

Next to the medicinal waters and the comfortable Georgian lifestyle that Bath offered, its diversions were a prime attraction - crucial to the spa's prosperity, holiday atmosphere and alluring image. More varied than commonly thought they ranged from highly structured entertainments to casual pastimes, from open-air pursuits to the indoor excitements of assemblies, plays and gaming tables. This volume, arranged in dictionary format, covers nearly 70 topics, including Assemblies, Auctions, Billiards, Boat Trips, Boxing, Breakfasting, Cards, Circus, Cockfighting, Coffee-houses, Concerts, Dancing, Dice, Exhibitions, Fireworks, Horse-racing, Lectures &c, Menageries, Pleasure Gardens, Poetry Contests, Puppet Shows, Raffles, Riding, Routs, Tennis and Theatre.

Compiled by Trevor Fawcett

Bath, Ruton, 1998: 96 pp in A5: £6: ISBN 0-9526326-1-6